# What Eve Must Know:

## Tactical Preparation for the Worst Day of Your Life

A book by

## Michael W. Weissberg

WHITE MOUNTAIN PUBLISHING CO.

MIAMI, FLORIDA

2011

# WHITE MOUNTAIN PUBLISHING CO.

## MIAMI, FLORIDA

Copyright 2011 by Michael Weissberg

Softcover, First edition


*Library of Congress Cataloging-in-Publication Data*

Weissberg, Michael.

      What Every Cop Must Know: Tactical Preparation for the Worst Day of Your Life by Michael Weissberg – 1$^{st}$ ed.

ISBN 10: 1494336782
ISBN 13: 978-1494336783

10 9 8 7 6 5 4 3 2 1

Book design by Michael Weissberg

Printed in the United States of America

Also by Michael Weissberg

Honor, Glory, Respect:
Conducting Police Funerals

The Firearm as a Martial Arts Weapon

Processing Environmental
Crime Scenes

Coming Soon from White Mountain
Publishing Company:

Off Duty: Concealed Weapons
Carry For Cops

Life is never what it seems, and every man must meet his destiny.

~ Dennis De Young

"Optimism is a good characteristic, but if carried to an excess, it becomes foolishness".

~ President Theodore Roosevelt

# About the Author

## Michael W. Weissberg

Sergeant Weissberg began his career as an educator in 1988. A graduate of the University of Miami, Weissberg holds Master's degrees in Education, Criminal Justice, and Psychology, from Nova Southeastern

University, Florida International University, and Northcentral University, as well as a Graduate Certificate in Criminal Justice Administration and Policy Making and a Certificate of Advanced Graduate Study in Industrial Organizational Psychology with a focus on Law Enforcement Management.

Professor Weissberg has taught on the undergraduate level at Miami Dade College, St. Thomas University, and Florida International University, and graduate school at Nova Southeastern University.

Sgt. Weissberg has served as a Police Officer, Crime Scene Investigator, Police Detective, Police Sergeant, and Acting Lieutenant.

# Acknowledgements

Grandmaster Bram Frank, a truly world-class martial artist, and possibly the best tactical knife teacher in the world today. Thank you for being my friend.

Master Sonia Waring, and Master Ryan Waring, Thanks for your help. Young Jude Waring (age 7), thanks for being a good boy and allowing your parents to teach without worrying if their son would tear the place up.

Ed Gottlieb, you are an inspired teacher. The photos you were in may save a cop's life.

Last, my son, Dean Bennett Bacon Weissberg, my awesome boy, and my wife, Erika B. Weissberg.

# Dedication

This book is dedicated to the Police Officers, Troopers, Law Enforcement Officers, and Federal Agents who allow us to sleep at night in peace, security, and freedom.

This book is dedicated to all fallen police officers everywhere; your sacrifice will never be forgotten.

To honor fallen Police Officers:

The National Law Enforcement Officers Memorial is the nation's monument to law enforcement officers who have died in the line of duty. Please donate.

If you would like to contribute by phone, please call 202-737-3400.

If you would like to contribute by Mail, please write:

NLEOMF
901 E Street NW, Suite 100
Washington, DC 20004-2025
info@nleomf.org

The Police Officer's Assistance Trust was founded in 1989 as a nonprofit support organization for the law enforcement community of Miami-Dade County, Florida. To make a donation contact POAT.

Police Officer's Assistance Trust
1030 NW 111 Avenue,
Miami, Florida 33172
305.594.6662
Email: poatoffice@msn.com

**A PORTION OF THE SALE OF THIS BOOK WILL BE DONATED TO POAT FOR THE FAMILIES OF OFFICRS KILLED IN LINE OF DUTY IN MIAMI-DADE COUNTY, FLORIDA.**

# Introduction

I have been to dozens of police funerals, and been an honor guard member, color guard member, casket guard, and a firing party member. I have been both a member and a commander. Many of these funerals have commonalities - the officer was killed feloniously, killed by his own mistakes, or killed by accident. Most could have been prevented.

All of the fallen left friends and family, coworkers and supporters, and all left a vacuum. You will read things here that may be unpopular, may make you angry, and may save your life. This book is for you; not because I know so much, because I don't. It's because we know so little, are our own worst enemies, and because we forget so much. As I said in my last book, The best we can do, is the least we can do.

Non soleus, (Never alone)
The Author

# Part 1: Mental Preparation

If I owe you a pound, I have a problem; but if I owe you a million, the problem is yours.

~ John Maynard Keynes

# Police Stress

# Before, During, and After the Job

The mass of men lead lives
of quiet desperation.

~ Henry David Thoreau

# Becoming a Police Officer

Welcome to the most stressful career in the country. Police stress knows no race color or gender. Stated plainly, it is illegal to discriminate in hiring based on age, disability, national origin, pregnancy, race, color, religion, sex, or sexual orientation. Everybody gets some stress here.

It is said that for every Police Officer in the United States, there were over 1,000 unsuccessful applicants rejected. This number is not officially attributed to anyone, and may be a manufactured number, but it has been perpetuated by and upon Law Enforcement for decades.

If more than one candidate makes it through the rigors of hiring, then the candidates are hired in order of the date of receipt of a completed application. It can take up to two years to traverse the hiring process, in order to be sent to the academy.

To illustrate the difficulty of getting a job in this field, one must examine the process.

## Becoming a Police Officer in Florida

In Florida, only certified candidates may be hired and put to work, or uncertified recruits may be hired and then given certification prior to working. The statutory authority for this is the Criminal Justice Standards & Training Commission (CJSTC) of the Florida Department of Law Enforcement (FDLE).

Prior to attending the Academy, Trainees must first pass a Test of Adult Basic Education (TABE), a basic abilities test (FBAT). This test is based on a job task analysis (JTA) in each of these subjects, adopted by the Criminal Justice Standards and Training Commission. After graduation from a CJSTC Academy, trainees seeking Florida certification as a law enforcement, correctional, or correctional probation officer must first pass the State Officer Certification Examination (SOCE).

Generally, by statute, to become employed as a certified law enforcement, correctional or correctional probation officer in Florida individuals must be at least 19 years of age, be a citizen of the United States, Have earned a high school graduate or equivalent , not have been convicted of any felony or of a misdemeanor involving perjury or false statement., never have received a dishonorable discharge from any of the Armed Forces of the United States, have good moral character, and have been fingerprinted by the employing agency with prints processed by the FDLE and the FBI. If these items are satisfied the next phase of hiring begins.

Prior to being hired, every candidate, even a certified and currently working Officer must pass a rigorous background check, including employment and credit check, a polygraph test which may take up to five hours, a psychological exam which may take up to five hours, one or more interviews, an examination of all files from previous agencies, a physical agility obstacle course/test, and a full medical exam with drug screen. Failure of any phase is an exit point. The trainee is now sent to the Academy.

At the basic recruit academy, every exam must be passes with an 80%. Failure of any exam is an exit point. Individuals who have completed the required Basic Recruit Training and passed the State Officer Certification Examination have four years from the start date of their Basic Recruit Training Program to become employed as an officer in Florida.

Once hired, every Officer must go through the Field Training Officer Program, based on the San Jose Model of the Field Training Officer Program. During this three month program, the trainee or probationer rides with a certified FTO who can pass or fail the trainee. Failure of any phase of FTO is an exit point.

Most departments have a probationary period of 9 to 18 months, during which an Officer can be terminated for any reason. It is easy to see why the average department is 10-20% understaffed at any given time, and qualified applicants are scarce. Discrimination is rare, and is usually rendered null by the rigor and regimentation of the long, arduous hiring process. Nepotism, cronyism, ageism, racism, sexism, and all of the other "isms" are not facilitated by a system that has so many examiners, instructors, proctors, and actors, from the Department, Academy, State, County, private and medical industries, and other entities. Discrimination is hiring is practically impossible, since no one has all the power. The final veto in hiring is held by the Chief of Police or Sheriff, but reason must be given and documented for a non-hire.

# Validity of Associate Selection Techniques

Muchinsky (2003) defines validity generalization as a concept that reflects the degree to which a predictive relationship empirically established in on context, spreads to another context, or stated more simply, if a process for hiring works for one company or division, and it works equally well for another company or division, then the validity can be said to be generalized. The validity of many techniques cannot be generalized as often as we would hope, and therefore, many fields have developed tests that do not really test what they purport to test.

The United States Border Patrol uses the "Entry-Level U.S. Border Patrol Logical Reasoning Test" as an entrance examination for pre-employment. In 1997, however, the Border Patrol had a test of artificial languages designed to see how easily a candidate would pick up on a new language, using nonsense, made-up language, to try to gauge how well a candidate would fare in the US Border Patrol / INS Spanish School. Needless to say, the validity and reliability of this test was In question, and that led to it being discontinued.

## Utility of Associate Selection Techniques

Utility is a concept that is underused, undervalued, and sorely needed. Utility deals with the economic cost and value of personnel decisions. Some tests are costly, and do not really test what they purport to (validity) and therefore may be a waste of money. In Law Enforcement, the TABE, FBAT, and Physical Agility Test (PAT) are paid for by the applicants, making the tests cost-effective for the agency. The Psychological, polygraph, medical, The State Officer Certification Examination, and drug screen are administered once

the TABE, FBAT, and Physical Agility
Test are passed.

# Motivation

In Law Enforcement, employees have several different motivators. There are three basic types of Police Officers: those who are motivated by money, those who are motivated to stay out of trouble, and those that are motivated to do a good job, and get recognition for that job.

Police Officers are supposed to answer calls for service, and when they have no calls, they are supposed to look for crime, and make arrests, or write tickets. Looking for traffic violators leads to uncovering other types of crimes. An active Patrol Officer is of great importance in a crime prevention program.

The Officers who write a lot of tickets and make a lot of arrests are doing just exactly what they are supposed to be doing, but what is their motivation for doing it?

There are some Police Officers who are money motivated. They make numerous arrests and write copious amounts of citations, in hopes that they will be subpoenaed to court on their off-duty time, and thus generate overtime pay. It is not uncommon for a midnight shift Police Officer who is active in traffic enforcement to receive $30,000 in overtime pay for going to court.

Some Police Officers are motivated by doing just enough work to be left alone by their superiors. These Police Officers have few or no arrests or citations in the beginning of a month, and pick up their production as the month wears on. Some Police Officers are simply motivated to do a good job, and give a good solid eight hours of work each time they work. These Police Officers are intrinsically motivated, and have a consistent level of arrests and citations year round.

Muchinsky (2003), put forth seven different theories of motivation, and several are obvious motivators in police work. According to Muchinsky (2003), Maslow's Hierarchy of Needs mentions five levels: Physiological

Needs, Safety Needs, Social Needs, Self-Esteem Needs, and Self Actualization. Police Officers go to work and maintain their jobs certainly for physiological and safety needs. But the social and self esteem needs are so firmly entrenched in Police socialization, that without them, policemen rarely succeed in retirement lives.

Skinner's theory of Reinforcement can be likened to the midnight shift patrol Police Officer who writes tickets or makes arrests, with the expectation of court overtime. The assignment to court via subpoena is a variable interval – there is no guarantee of court overtime, since most of the time the person cited simply pays the ticket by mail.

By the luck of the draw, some motorists will elect to take the ticket to court, and in doing so, cause the Police Officer to draw overtime pay for court attendance. In a 1995 investigation by the Miami Herald newspaper, this was termed "collars for dollars".

Most patrol Officers work on a Self-Regulation Theory. The average patrol Officer may assume that turning in forty citations and four arrests per calendar month will satisfy the patrol sergeant. The average Officer will write only enough tickets to get to the point of "stasis", where the monthly or annual performance evaluation will give a satisfactory rating.

If the Officer has two or three "big ticket" cases, such as a DUI or a multi-car crash, he may write many tickets, and may "take it easy" for the rest of the week, so as not to upset the balance and draw attention to himself – if it possible to write 50 or 60 tickets, then why doesn't the Officer do that every month?

The Police Officer that always seems to lead the squad in arrests and citations is probably going to get the Officer of the Month award several times. This Officer is alert, awake, and notices crime as it happens. This Police Officer may "discover" a burglary in progress and catch the subject in the middle of the crime. This Police Officer gets rewards and may get promoted rapidly.

Other Police Officers may disparage this Officer as being someone who is "kissing up" to management. This Police Officer is motivated by the reward or the possibility of the reward, and is subscribing to "Goal Setting Theory".

The Police Officer's goal is to catch criminals, write tickets, and make arrests. The Police Officer knows that he does not have to work as hard as he does, but the title or plaque he gets every few months motivates him to do his best, rather than read a book under a tree or just stare into space for a while rather than go "hunting" for a ticket or an arrest.

Police Officers are lauded as heroes for going into situations that most people would never go into – entering a dark alley at night, or checking out weird noises in someone's back yard, and many people would not and could not do this dangerous and difficult job.

Police Officers are often lumped into a group, but we forget that each Officer is an individual, with different motivators, and different theories of motivation apply for each.

Motivation is an area that is so important, an entire industry has grown up around it. Millions are spent annually on books, speakers, programs, and organizations, to figure out how to motivate employees.

Motivation is explained by Champoux (2006) as psychological processes that cause the voluntary actions that are goal oriented. Abraham Maslow's Hierarchy of Needs Theory and Clayton P. Alderfer's Existence, Relatedness, Growth Need Hierarchy (ERG theory) are similar, and can explain some of the basis for the motivation of fulfilling desires and needs. One can compare and contrast the theories, and although there are differences between them, one must remember that

Alderfer's ERG Theory is based on Maslow's Hierarchy of Needs Theory.

## Maslow

In 1943 Abraham Maslow proposed a Theory of Human Needs. In Maslow's theory, there are five levels of human needs, which are: physiological, security, the need to belong, esteem needs, and self-actualization. According to Huitt (2007) prior to Maslow, researchers generally focused separately on such factors as biology, achievement, or power to explain what energizes, directs, and sustains human behavior.

Maslow (1943) stated that physiological needs include breathing, food, sexual activity, and homeostasis. Animal needs include food, water, cover, and space. According to Huitt (2007), Maslow posited a hierarchy of human needs based on two groupings: deficiency needs and growth needs. Within the deficiency needs, each lower need must be met before moving to the next higher level. Once each of these needs has been satisfied, if at some future time a deficiency is detected, the individual will act to remove the deficiency.

Safety and Security needs include personal security, financial security, health and well-being, and a safety net against accidents/illness and the adverse impacts. After physiological and safety needs are fulfilled, the third layer of Maslow's needs is social. This aspect of the hierarchy involves emotionally-based relationships in general, such as friendship, fellowship, intimacy, and family support. In the fourth level, esteem, Maslow stresses that positive self-respect is based on earned respect. The final level, the fifth level, self-actualization is the final need that can be fulfilled when lower level needs have been satisfied. The motivation to realize one's own maximum potential and possibilities is what makes up self-actualization.

Daniels (2001) suggested that Maslow's ultimate conclusion that the highest levels of self-actualization are transcendent in their nature may be one of his most important contributions to the study of human behavior and motivation.

Huitt (2007) claims that Maslow recognized that not everyone followed his proposed hierarchy. While a variety of personality dimensions might be considered as related to motivational needs, one of the most often cited is that of introversion and extroversion. Norwood (1999) proposed that Maslow's hierarchy can be used to describe the kinds of information individual's seek at different levels of development. For example, individuals at the lowest level seek coping information in order to meet their basic needs.

Information that is not directly connected to helping a person meet his or her needs in a very short time span is simply left unattended. Individuals at the safety level need helping information. They seek to be assisted in seeing how they can be safe and secure. Enlightening information is sought by individuals seeking to meet their belongingness needs. Quite often this can be found in books or other materials on relationship development. Empowering information is sought by people at the esteem level. They are looking for information on how their egos can be developed. Finally, people in the growth levels of cognitive, aesthetic, and self-actualization seek edifying information.

## Alderfer

The ERG Theory of Clayton P. Alderfer is a model that appeared in 1969 in an article entitled "An Empirical Test of a New Theory of Human Need", In a reaction to Maslow's Hierarchy of Needs, Alderfer distinguishes three categories of human needs that influence worker's behavior; existence, relatedness and growth.

These ERG Theory categories are: existence needs: physiological and safety needs such as hunger, thirst and sex relatedness needs: social and external esteem such as involvement with family, friends, co-workers and employers, and growth needs: internal esteem and self actualization such as desires to be creative, productive and to complete meaningful tasks.

This seems to be a re-ordination and re-classification of Maslow's Theory, and might have been discounted completely if it were not for one item: contrarily to Maslow's tenet that access to the higher levels of his hierarchy required satisfaction in the lower level needs, according to Alderfer the three ERG contain no ordination whatsoever.

Alternate Theories of Motivation

Nohria, Lawrence, and Wilson (2001) provide a sociological-biological theory of motivation that people have four basic needs: to acquire objects and experiences; to bond with others in long-term relationships of mutual care and commitment, to learn and make sense of the world and of ourselves; and to defend ourselves, our loved ones, beliefs and resources from harm.

The Institute for Management Excellence (2001) suggests there are nine basic human needs: security, adventure, freedom, exchange, power, expansion, acceptance, community, and expression.

According Frederick Herzberg, the Two Factor Theory (or Motivation-Hygiene Theory) of people is influenced by two factors. Satisfaction and psychological growth was a factor of motivation factors. Dissatisfaction was a result of hygiene factors.

Herzberg developed this motivation theory during his investigation of 200 accountants and engineers in the USA. Besides The Two Factor Theory, Frederick

Herzberg is also known sometimes for his acronym KITA, which has been translated as a "kick in the Ass!" Herzberg said that KITA does not produce motivation but only movement. Herzberg (1968) stated later, that the surest and least circumlocuted way of getting someone to do something is the KITA.

According to Value Based Management, Victor Vroom stated that the Expectancy Theory of deals with motivation and management. Vroom's theory assumes that behavior results from conscious choices among alternatives whose purpose it is to maximize pleasure and minimize pain.

Together with Edward Lawler and Lyman Porter, Vroom suggested that the relationship between people's behavior at work and their goals was not as simple as was first imagined by other scientists. Vroom realized that an employee's performance is based on individual's factors such as personality, skills, knowledge, experience and abilities.

# Summary

One cannot be reckless and immediately discount Maslow's classic theory in favor of a "new and improved" theory posited by Vroom, Herzberg, Alderfer, or others who had the opportunity to read Maslow. Maslow will always have the role of pioneer since there were few if any theories before his in this area.

Hofstede (1980) goes so far as to say that many of the differences in employee motivation, management styles, and organizational structures of complies throughout the world can be traced to differences in culture and programming, suggesting that Maslow and Alderfer may not be as universal as initially thought. One must keep in mind that these theories are theories, and not rules, and as we progress, these theories might be changed, modified, or eventually even discarded.

It is the job of a supervisor to provide the framework or context that an employee works within, and the job of that manager to rate and evaluate that employee. This is a commonality in the workplace. Good performance is supposed to be recognized, and rewarded, and poor performance is supposed to be corrected, and remediated. This is commonly accepted, but in reality, the obverse is sometimes true.

There is a common joke that is called the "pattern of failure", which delineates an ordinate schedule for a process in organizations: enthusiasm for the goal, disillusionment with the progress, search for the guilty, persecution of the innocent, and praise for the non-participants.

Humor is often made up of truisms, and no one is better at ferreting out the truth in organizations than "Dilbert" cartoonist Scott Adams. Every Industrial Organizational Psychologist knows the Dilbert-style managers, and every employee does too.

Performance appraisal is an opportunity for management to foster quality and excellence when done right; performance appraisal is an opportunity for management to foster the "Dilbert syndrome" and prove Adams right when done wrong.

# Stress Management

It can be argued that when organizations utilize stress management programs to help workers deal with stress, rather than design programs to make work less stressful, organizations are treating the symptoms rather than addressing the causes.

Muchinsky (2003) mentions that stress management initiatives include onsite physical fitness, exercise, meditation, and time management programs. But stressors caused by the organization can be lessened. It is therefore proposed that Law Enforcement agencies follow both the spirit and the letter of the law, and begin to work toward reducing police stress, for the good of the officers, the agencies, and the communities they serve.

Police stress is a silent killer. The number of police officer who die early from stress induced heart attacks and strokes is staggering. Police Officers must work in an environment that makes it necessary to complete a shift without physical, mental, emotional, or legal trouble.

One Union, the Police Benevolent Association of Florida, offers disciplinary Representation, in the form of full-time and retained attorneys to handle discipline cases, as well as your decertification cases before the Criminal Justice Standards and Training Commission, an attorney to represent you at the scene of an on-duty shooting or serious injury, and an attorney if named as a defendant in any civil or criminal action arising out of duties as a law enforcement officer.

Finn (1997) believes that the causes of police stress are supervisory style, field training officer programs, critical incident counseling, lack of command support after critical incidents, shift work, and job assignments shift schedules, job assignments, and the scheduling of court time.

Most police departments work using a 40 hour work week, with a "five-eight" plan, meaning the officer works 5 eight-hour shifts. There are normally three platoons, Alpha, Bravo and Charlie. The Alpha Platoon is 6 AM to 2 PM, the Bravo Platoon is 2 PM to 10 PM, and the Charlie Platoon is 10 PM to 6 AM.

In many departments there are night differentials, extra pay for working in the dark, which is more stressful, less healthful, and less desirable. A 5% Bravo shift differential and a 10% Charlie shift differential is common. Most departments bid for shift by seniority, so veterans typically wind up on Alpha, unless they are motivated by the differential pay to go to Bravo or Charlie. Some officers move to another shift to avoid an undesirable supervisor.

Some departments use a "four-ten" plan where officers work 4 ten-hour shifts, in order to get another day off. In order to save money, some departments use the "3-twelve", which forces a 12 hour shift on officers, with different days off each week, and the officer must work an extra four hour day once a week, or an extra eight once each two weeks, to meet the forty hour week.

Sundermeier (2009) discusses twelve-hour shifts that were implemented on a trial basis by the Lincoln Police Department in Lincoln, Nebraska. Areas of concern were identified prior to implementation, including officer fatigue, court scheduling, and the impact the schedule might have on case management and quality of service.

Some benefits and prohibitions were not discussed by Sundermeier, a Captain and obvious proponent of the 12 hour shift (and one who undoubtedly "drives" a desk and does not go to court): for an officer who has to travel 30 minutes or more to get to and from work, fewer days means less hours of travel per week. More time off with family, and every other weekend off may sweeten the pot for a rookie officer, but a veteran who has weekends off will lose two weekends off per month. For those officers used to working 10 hours, the 12 takes less adjustment and it means and one less day working.

The drawbacks are that if something happens late in the shift, such as a "hot call", the 12 hour shift becomes a 16-240 hour day very quickly. For officers with a family, it is harder to attend sports or school events for kids (what Muchinsky (2003) calls a work/family conflict).

For those officers assigned to Charlie Shift (nights) can seem very long, and court can make it much longer. If the officer is grumpy or having a "bad day", 12 hours can be enough to push one to the point of violence or unnecessary use of force.

The stressful nature of police shift work is that Charlie shift officers must go to court on their off-duty time, which impinges on family time, but allows for more overtime money for the money-motivated officer.

The concept of going to school under a tuition reimbursement program is almost impossible for an active Charlie shift officer who goes to court several times a week. The twelve hour day makes court almost unbearable.

Bravo shift officers will get some court time, and some time will be on-duty, which is seen as positive or negative, depending on if the officer values overtime money or time off.

Since Finn (1997) believes that some of the causes of police stress are supervisory style, shift work, and job assignments shift schedules, job assignments, and the scheduling of court time, it is obvious that officers will be scheduled to work with supervisors they do not like, and will either lose overtime in some circumstances, causing financial hardship, or will be forced to attend court during a time they do not want to, causing family problems.

If a case goes to trial, it is not unusual in some jurisdictions to be in court for eight hours. Imagine a

Charlie shift officer works from 10 PM to 6 AM, gets off tired, then has to drive to court. Court overtime begins at the calendar call time, so for an 8AM court call, the tired officer must wait, unpaid, in his car or in the building. A jury must be picked using the "Voir Dire" system (Latin for "to seek, to say" or "to seek the truth"), then the prosecution and defense must make opening statements, and the court takes recesses and a lunch break.

The officer may not get to take the stand for several hours. If the officer's testimony does not end until 5 PM, the officer caught in rush hour, may not make it home until 6 or 7 PM.

The officer can then chose to shave and shower, eat, or sleep, and at 9 PM begin to prepare for work again at 10 PM. Stress, fatigue, and hunger all combine, and augmented by and angry spouse, disappointed children, lack of exercise and an abundance of fast food, are a recipe for an early grave.

Anecdotally, the case of "Captain Tony" can be illustrative. Captain Tony began police work in 1968. This officer worked from age 22 upon his graduation from the academy.

Captain Tony served 41 years, and died in his sleep at age 63, after giving two-thirds of his life to the community; Captain Tony never got to see a dollar of his well-earned pension, didn't get to enjoy retirement with his wife of four decades, and left many things unsaid and undone.

Captain Tony was in better physical shape than the average 63 year-old, and made enough money as a Police Captain to not have unusual money woes. Captain Tony was cremated and eulogized inn a in a small but dignified ceremony that the entire fifty officer department turned out for.

Captain Tony served for forty-one years; excluding officers, fewer than forty-one mourners attended. This is an actual case of a Florida

Police Officer, only the last name has been withheld.

## 10 Deadly Errors

It is unknown, who actually authored the "10 Deadly Errors", but they came out around 1975, and are generally credited to Los Angeles Police Department Homicide Investigator Pierce R. Brooks; they are posted in most police stations and police academies, and taught in them as well. These errors are even quoted in the FBI Law Enforcement Bulletin, the police journal published by the Federal Bureau of Investigation.

They are: lack of concentration, tombstone courage, not enough rest, taking a bad position, not heeding the danger signs, failure to watch the hands of a suspect, relaxing too soon on a scene, improper handcuffing, no search or bad search of a subject, and dirty or inoperative weapon or equipment. Besides the lack of rest, one does not have to be an officer to know that the other nine signs could also be signs of suicidal behavior, or a wish to go out as a hero, gunned down by a felon, rather than be seen as a coward or psychotic. We must do a better job of protecting our protectors, even sometimes from themselves.

## Proposed Changes

Changes are proposed herein in the areas of Physical Training and Portal to Portal, Sleep Deprivation, Powernaps, and Microsleeps, and Mental and Emotional Fitness Training.

## Physical Training and Portal to Portal

The average police department does not have a gym for officers to exercise. It is recommended that all police departments obtain gym facilities through grants or fund matching, and those that lack money or space, should either partner with community centers, universities, or fire departments, or purchase gym memberships at private gyms.

Some departments allow one hour for working out per shift. This should be expanded to all departments. In Florida, SWAT team members get one hour per day of workout time or pay via the "Garcia Amendment" Fair Labor Standards Act since physical fitness is a job requirement; but isn't it a requirement of all law enforcements officers?

In Dade Co. v. Alvarez, Several current and former members of the Metro-Dade Police Department's Special Response Team sued Miami-Dade County under the Fair Labor Standards Act, 29 U.S.C. §§ 201, *et seq.,* (FLSA), to recover overtime pay for off- duty hours spent performing physical fitness training. After a jury verdict in their favor, the district court entered judgment for the SRT officers.

In Dade Co. v. Alvarez , at the conclusion of trial, the district court submitted a special verdict to the jury, which made the following factual determinations: the SWAT Officer's off-duty physical training or exercise is required or controlled by the County; the SWAT Officer's off-duty physical training or exercise is performed predominantly for the benefit of the County; the SWAT Officer's off-duty physical training is an integral and indispensable part of their principal activities as SRT officers; and that Miami-Dade County either knew, or showed reckless disregard, that its conduct violated the FLSA.

Following the ruling, and using the so-called "Garcia Rule" or "Garcia Amendment", SWAT, Motorcycle Officers ("Motormen") and Canine (K9) Handler-Officers are now paid for things like working out to maintain fitness levels, bathing, feeding, and caring for police dogs, and maintaining police motorcycles, in accord with the Fair Labor Standards Act Of 1938.

It is proposed that all officers get time to train and to work out, and for "donning and doffing" an industry term meaning to pack and unpack their cars, and put on the 20-30 pounds of equipment an officer needs to wear (FLSA coverage by §§4(a)(1) and (2) of the Portal-to-Portal Act).

This would ensure fit officers who do not feel "put upon" by performing acts twice daily that take up to an hour, without compensation.

## Sleep Deprivation, Powernaps, and Microsleeps

Compare and contrast Police Officers with Firefighters. Firefighters in Miami-Dade County are issued a pillow, blanket, and bed by Miami-Dade County. Police Officers found to be sleeping on duty can be disciplined, terminated, and or decertified by The Florida Department of Law Enforcement's (FDLE) Criminal Justice Standards Training Commission (CJSTC).

Officers who crash their police vehicles due to working tired, a condition sometimes caused by the work itself, can be disciplined or terminated. Officers may be forced to work extra shifts due to "hold-overs", mandatory overtime to meet minimum staffing when other officers call out sick, or for storms, disasters, riots, or affray.

Some officers work in an exhausted state where they experience "microsleeps", mini 1-30 second "naps" where they fall asleep while driving.

The International Classification of Sleep Disorders (ICSD) is a primary diagnostic, epidemiological and coding resource for clinicians and researchers in the field of sleep and sleep medicine. It is produced by the American Academy of Sleep Medicine, and states that a "microsleep" is an episode of sleep which may last for a fraction of a second or up to thirty seconds, often, as the result of sleep deprivation or mental fatigue.

If Police Officers are going to be forced to work ten twelve, fourteen, or more hours without proper sleep, then it is proposed that officers be given the same sleep space and gear as their firefighter cohorts, for a sixty minute "powernap" after ten hours of continuous duty caused by combinations of shift work, hold-overs, off-duty jobs, and court time.

# Subcultures in Police Organizations

The reason subcultures form is for protection, well-being, and camaraderie are all reasons that subcultures form. Sometimes groups of people who share common characteristics will be drawn to each other.

Street gangs, prison gangs, hate groups, and terrorist organizations are just some of the negative results of subcultures forming. Subcultures can be formal or informal. Some groups go as far as printing hats and shirts, throwing holiday parties, or having special events.

While these events can galvanize groups of employees and can foster close work groups and working relationships, they can also serve to polarize workplaces by their exclusionary characteristics.

Sometimes being a part of a subculture can even lead to employment or promotional opportunities. Some examples are college fraternities such as Pi Kappa Alpha, Sigma Chi and Zeta Beta Tau, certain Universities such as The Citadel, West Point, and Yale, higher education organizations, such as Phi Beta Kappa and Yale University's Skull and Bones, or organizations, such as the BPOE Elks, Rotarians, or Masons. Letting a supervisor or manager know that they share membership can make for a favorable impression, which can lead to new opportunities not open to others. Joining an organization because you know a boss is a member is not out of line, if you are low key about it.

Becoming a Freemason was a choice I made because I wanted to be a member and enjoy the brotherhood of Masonry. Later, I found out that many good, benevolent, powerful people were also Masons.

## Implications for New Employees

Depending on the organization and type of work, subcultures can be beneficial to downright deadly for new hires; it might be easy to dismiss that statement as dramatic, but with workplace violence and hate crime being examined on a micro and macro level, it is possible that simply being discriminated against may not be a new hire's biggest worry, if that person is a minority, Muslim, or homosexual.

Violence against minorities, Muslims, and homosexuals can be shocking in its voracity. Since 09/11/2009, even being suspected of being Muslim can have deadly consequences. The resurgence of Skinhead and Neo-Nazi hate groups can make being identified or misidentified as a homosexual a deadly event.

## Subcultures as Positives

As horrible as the negative consequences can be, the benefits of subcultures for new hires can be equally beneficial at the other end of the spectrum. Gagliardi (1986) found that organizations with strong cultures are capable of only limited change because members are especially resistant to changing those strongly held and widely shared values.

Associations for Hispanics, Blacks, females, and other protected groups, can give succor and acceptance to new hires. Boisnier and Chatman (2002) state that subcultures can permit an organization to generate varied responses to the environment without necessarily destroying its internal coherence. Subcultures may provide the flexibility and responsiveness that a unitary culture may limit.

Test answers for promotional exams, and advice on how to survive a certain supervisor's wrath, or secrets to getting away with shortchanging the organization, can be shared and passed on to employees who would not normally be privy to this information without first serving months or years in that organization.

Boisnier and Chatman (2002) not that subcultures have certain properties that can even strengthen an organization's overall organizational culture; subcultures often emerge in response to changing demands and can serve as an outlet for members to express conflict and dissent arising during turbulent times.

Most Law Enforcement Agencies have several subcultures that form regardless of the agency size, locale, or surrounding area.

Boisnier and Chatman (2002) say that organizational subcultures may be based on membership in various groups such as departments, workgroups, and teams; levels of hierarchies, such as management versus support staff; professional and occupational affiliations. Hispanic and Black Police Officers have the Hispanic Police Officer Association (HPOA) and the National Organization of Black Law Enforcement (NOBLE), respectively. According to NOBLE, the "NOBLE Purpose" is to unify

Black Law Enforcement Officers at executive and command levels.

According to HPOA, among the things that HPOA has been actively involved in include the recruitment of Hispanics, assisting new recruits and heir families, providing career enhancement training to its members, taking a leadership in the Hispanic communities, and establishing scholarships for students. The HPOA has a prep class for Sergeant that is free for members, and hundreds of Officers join for this benefit alone.

Subcultures also form based on assignment. Detectives, for example, do not often mix with patrol officers, due to operational differences and a pseudo class distinction. Tactical Officers (SWAT, SRT, ERT) tend to stay apart from everyone, and have their organization, the National Tactical Officer Association (NTOA).

The founder of NTOA hoped to provide a communications link between SWAT units throughout the United States and, later, other countries. All prospective members of the NTOA must meet prescribed membership criteria.

There are similar organizations for Canine Handlers, Field Training Officers, Crime Prevention Officers, Crime Scene Investigators, Homicide Detectives, Auto Theft Investigators, Fixed Wing Aircraft and Rotary Pilots, Motorcycle Officers, Police Divers, and Drug Recognition Experts and DUI Officers.

Management tends to disassociate from line officers, and ranking officers in middle and upper management join organizations such as the Dade Chief's Association, The Florida Sheriff's Association, and the International Organization of Chiefs of Police.

On the other end of the strata, Probationary Police Officers (PPO), rookies, and academy trainees, are often out of the loop on social events, and have no support system whatsoever.

County Sheriffs, Municipal Police Officers, State Police and Troopers, and Federal Agents all have their own organizations, and rarely mix with each other in a social setting. Even neighboring municipalities enjoy a healthy rivalry and when attending awards ceremonies for Kiwanis, MADD, Rotarians, and the like, sit only with members of their own departments, and then, separated in groups by race or assignment.

One might think this is in direct conflict with the "thin blue line" and the "blue wall of silence" that was made famous by Joseph Wambough books and Steven Bochco television series, but once outside entities begin to entreat into the affairs of law enforcement, the Officers, Detectives, Managers, and Specialized Units close ranks and retreat from outside scrutiny and influences.

Law Enforcement is a subculture all its own. Ask any Officer and they will say that they feel trial by a "jury of their peers" is a humorous term, since their peers are Law Enforcement.

With typical machismo, they will state without deviation that "once you look down the barrel of a loaded gun, hold a dead baby in your arms, or scrape a teenaged brain off a sidewalk, then you will be qualified to judge me" or words to that effect. This is the very reason for the line that they draw to separate themselves from the public, that often results in a suicide and divorce rate well above that of the civilian populace, and a life expectancy well below.

# Law Enforcement Ethics

Some fields have ethics and ethical codes that govern behavior. Lawyers, clergymen, accountants, psychologists, and doctors all have ethical considerations in their jobs. Doctors and hospitals even have ethical committees to decide what ethics are and if ethical considerations have been violated.

In police work, ethics are so ingrained in training and in job performance, that there is no need for committees to decide what ethics are or if they have been violated. Each Officer knows what is right and wrong, ethical and unethical, and does not need further definition.

Examples would be stealing from a crime scene, using a data terminal to find information on an ex-spouse, falsifying a report, or perjuries in testifying. These acts are all illegal, and also unethical, so the Officer needs no guidance.

Some ethical violations are not illegal; in Florida, "reckless driving" is a criminal citation, and therefore arrestable. Writing tickets for both "reckless driving" and "careless driving" is considered to be unethical and called "stacking charges", because "careless driving" is a lesser included offense to "reckless driving".

Every episode of "reckless driving" contains "careless driving". Officers who stack charges in order to "punish" violators who have annoyed them, or to "pad their statistics" have committed ethical violations, but not legal violations (crimes).

Similarly, every burglary contains a trespass (lesser included offense), so to charge someone who breaks into a house with both trespass to the property (curtilage) and burglary to the dwelling (house), has stacked the charges.

There are numerous other examples that exist, which are unethical but not illegal. An Officer, who has stacked charges, will not be disciplined; the extra charge will be dropped by the Assistant State Attorney, and if questioned, the Officer would usually claim ignorance or mistake.

According to the Florida Department of Law Enforcement, ethics violations in the State of Florida are handled by The Criminal Justice Standards & Training Commission (CJSTC).

Established under Florida Statute, Chapter 943, is an independent policy making body that ensures that Florida's citizens are served by a qualified, well trained, competent, and ethical law enforcement community. The 19 member Commission is comprised of criminal justice and community leaders as set forth in Florida Statute.

The CJSTC is responsible for creating entry-level curricula and certification testing for criminal justice officers in Florida, establishing minimum standards for employment and certification and revoking the certification of officers who fail to maintain these minimum standards of conduct.

The Professional Compliance Section is responsible for investigating allegations of misconduct by officers, training school instructors, and Commission-certified criminal justice training schools for possible disciplinary or denial of certification action by the Commission, and ensures that due-process is observed throughout Commission proceedings.

## Ethics in Government

In Florida, the "Sunshine Law" calls for "government in the sunshine", meaning there are no papers, meetings, or findings that are not a matter of public record. Florida State Statute 119.01 states "General state policy on public records - It is the policy of this state that all state, county, and municipal records are open for personal inspection and copying by any person.

Providing access to public records is a duty of each agency." According to the Florida Attorney General, Florida's Government-in-the-Sunshine Law was created in 1967. The Sunshine Law establishes a basic right of access to most meetings of boards, commissions and other governing bodies of state and local governmental agencies or authorities.

The State of Florida also has an Ethics Commission. The Florida Commission on Ethics is a nine-member group, with a staff of twenty employees located in the state capitol, that serves as the "guardian" of the standards of conduct for officers and employees of Florida and is an independent commission responsible for investigating and issuing public reports on complaints of breaches of public trust by elected officials, public officers, and employees.

The Commission also renders legally binding advisory opinions interpreting the ethics laws and implements the State's financial disclosure laws. The Commission, by majority vote, interprets and applies Florida's ethics laws by taking action on complaints, recommending penalties, and issuing legal opinions.

The "Code of Ethics for Public Officers and Employees" adopted by the Legislature is in Chapter 112 of the Florida Statutes. One of the goals of the Code is to promote the public interest and maintain the respect of the people for their government.

The Code is also intended to ensure that public officials govern themselves independently and impartially, and not use their offices for private gain other than compensation provided by law. The Code also seeks to avoid the creation of unnecessary barriers to public service. Standards of ethics conduct and disclosures are applicable to public officers, employees, candidates, lobbyists, and others in Florida State and local government. The Code is not applicable to Judges.

The ethical standards for Judges of Florida's judicial branch are contained in the Code of Judicial Conduct, adopted by the Florida Supreme Court.. Sections 350.031 - 350.05 & 350.0605, Florida Statutes, contain standards of conduct that apply particularly to members and employees of the Public Service Commission and to members of the Public Service Commission Nominating Council.

Other laws governing ethics exist in Florida. Chapter 287, Florida Statutes, contains standards relating to State motor vehicles and aircraft; when possible violations are reported by the Comptroller, the Ethics Commission has the authority to investigate suspected violations. Section 11.062(2), Florida Statutes, prohibits certain State and Local agencies from using public funds to retain lobbyists before the legislative or executive branches of State government and gives the Ethics Commission the authority to investigate complaints alleging a violation of this standard.

The positive effects of ethics in police work and government are qualitative, not quantitative. When Police Officers act in an ethical manner, and have a reputation for truthful testimony, punctuality, and honesty, court appearances go more smoothly.

Attorneys for the defense often plan their strategies based on which officer is going to be called to testify. Officers who are perceived as honest and knowledgeable by juries are believed, and the defendant is more often found guilty. The defense attorney is more likely to advise the client to take a plea arrangement rather than go to trial with an Officer who is well liked and believed by the jury.

Another positive effect is that judges know the Officers who appear frequently in their courtrooms. When an Officer represents something as factual, the judge can believe that, and frequently finds for the State in matters of pretrial motions, notices of expiration, Motions in Limine, Metier Motions, Arthur Hearings, and other motions and hearings that hinge upon the judge, who is trier of law, acting as trier of fact, in pretrial motions.

Organizations are like organisms. Organizations have systems. Treating a group of individuals, in an organization, as a single organism, is akin to treating the body as the sum of the parts. The body of an otter, whale, or hippopotamus contains millions of cells, each with a specific function; that body is made up of systems; reproductive, digestive, and so on, which make up the animal; an organization woks this way as well.

Organizations have a culture, which can be shaped by a leader. Employees learn the culture of the organization via a process known as organizational socialization. The new employee must learn the core values, mission, vision, and purpose of the organization, and participate toward achieving that goal, to be successful in that employment.

Certain behaviors are required of the individual for the good of that organization. These behaviors are monitored by supervisors and managers. Cable & Parsons (2001) know that interviewer and applicant decisions help to calculate person–organization fit, the person–organization fit may evolve via organizational socialization.

Champoux (2006) states that there are three stages of organizational socialization: choice: anticipatory socialization, colloquially referred to as "getting in", entry/encounter, colloquially referred to as "breaking in", and change: metamorphosis colloquially referred to as "settling in".

The relationships among the stages, is simple, in that these aforementioned stages link, with the result of one stage becoming the factor of the next stage. Another way to refer to this, is "expectations", "reality", and "taking on the role".

People must adjust to their new environment, coworkers, bosses, and tasks. An employee is expected to be a "team player" and to be "on board" with the program proffered, whatever it may be. Anakwe & Greenhaus (1999) know that when employees join the organization, they need to learn and understand the way things are done within their work units/groups that is consistent with that of other relevant employees.

An employee who fits in and works toward the goals and objectives is rewarded with a chance to continue employment, advance, and receive positive evaluations. An employee who does not fit in and obstructs the goals and objectives is denied a chance to continue employment, advance, and receive positive evaluations.

The negative effects of not fitting in include a poor work resume, loss of income and with it possible loss of sustenance or homestead, poor credit, and a social stigma.

There are socialization processes happening within each stage. The "getting in" stage involves a person trying to enter the organization. Champoux (2006) mentions organizational socialization begins here, often with recruitment. The person's expectations and beliefs develop, and the person begins to have a concept of the organization. This concept may not be realistic. The recruiters may posit an inflated image, which cannot be maintained; the prospective employee may be disappointed when these "pie in the sky" images fail to develop. In the "breaking in" stage, the employee finds out how realistic these impressions were.

Champoux (2006) realizes that the new hire is eager to make friends and impress; a false image of the employee may be conveyed, that cannot be maintained in the long term. The employee must learn the ropes.

In the 1700's, a midshipman in the Royal Navy would take years to learn what each individual rope did in the adjustment of sails, and what that rope was for; an employee may have only days or weeks to "learn the ropes". A new hire can be given conflicting messages, and conflicting expectations. Orientations, mentorships, apprenticeships, and indoctrination programs can assist the new employee.

Champoux (2006) stands for the proposition that the "settling in" stage is more gradual than dynamic, and involves the employee beginning to feel comfortable in the new role.

Some organizations have ceremonies and rituals at this stage. A graduation party may take place in some organizations or work groups. An anniversary pin may be issued. Unsuccessful transitions can lead to rebellious behavior, which can lead to termination.

Taormina (1994) created an instrument to assist with socialization in organizations. Taormina identified four social-psychological factors that were theorized to influence employee perceptions of their socialization at work: training; understanding; co-worker support; and prospects for the future. Based on these factors, The Organizational Socialization Inventory (OSI) was created as a quantitative measure of socialization in organizations. The OSI is intended for general use in a variety of organizational settings.

Chao et al.'s (1994) six-part content areas of socialization (CAS) measure, can be employed as well. Six socialization dimensions (performance proficiency, politics, language, people, organizational goals/values, and history) are used to determine relationships between learning particular features of a job/organization and the process and outcomes of socialization.

A precursor to Chao and Taormina was Van Maanen (1978), who identified 7 dimensions or strategies of socialization: The 7 dimensions are as follows: formal–

informal, individual–collective, sequential–nonsequential, fixed–variable, tournament–contest, serial–disjunctive, and investiture–divestiture.

Van Maanen said that people in a state of transition are in an anxiety-producing situation and are motivated to reduce this anxiety by learning the functional and social requirements of their new role as rapidly as possible. The learning that takes place does not occur in a social vacuum strictly on the basis of the official and available versions of the job requirements; the stability and productivity of any organization depends largely on the way new hires carry out their tasks.

Law Enforcement Applications

Chao et al, (1994) remind us that an individual's success may well be rooted in gaining information regarding formal and informal work relationships and power structures within the organization. In law enforcement, this is especially important in the first 90 days. Ashforth & Saks (1996) state that Individuals are particularly susceptible to influence during role transitions, because they are uncertain as to the requirements of their new role. Listening to bad advice can be disastrous.

A new officer must go through a three month program known as the "San Antonio model" of the Field Training Officer Program. Failure to navigate this program successfully often results in termination, and in police work, terminated employees often are unemployable.

The Field Training Officer is of equal rank to the new hire officer, or probationary police officer (PPO), but is often "hooked up" with the Field training Sergeant, Field Training Lieutenant, and other high ranking officials. It is not uncommon for a hoary old FTO to have "FTO'd" the Chief of Police. This FTO may have a direct link to any senior management official.

Anakwe & Greenhaus (1999) mention that knowledge and acceptance of organization's culture is important. Knowledge reflects employees' understanding of the organization's culture. Acceptance relates to how fully the employees have internalized the culture of the organization. Every new employee has to be familiar with the organizational culture.

In police work, the culture varies from department to department, but some things are accepted norms across the board: back up fellow officers, transmit damaging information in person or on the cell phone (not over the radio), and learn to say things in writing and verbally that will not damage other officers in internal investigations (I didn't see the episode, I was writing a report at the time).

While it may not be wholly ethical to act in this manner, officers who do not pick up the "lingo" will often be outcast. Ostroff & Kozlowski (1992) found that the acquisition of information affects the relationship between organizational socialization tactics and key socialization outcomes in terms of attitudes.

This shows how rapidly a new employee can adjust during organizational socialization. This backs up Van Maanen's idea that new hires are motivated to reduce this anxiety by learning the functional and social requirements of their new role as quickly as possible.

During this three month "settling in" stage, the new hire learns the job, and at the end, when the employee beginning to feel comfortable in the new role, there is a test, after which the new officer is allowed to drive alone and take calls alone, write tickets, initiate citizen contacts or traffic stops, and make arrests alone. Nine to twelve months later, the PPO finished probation and becomes an Officer.

Four years later, the Officer drops the moniker "rookie" and can be referred to as a "veteran". In LAPD terms, a PPO is an "Officer one", an FTO is an "Officer two", and a veteran is an "Officer three". Most departments do not have these grades.

After three years of service, an officer receives a stripe or "hash mark" to wear on the long sleeve uniform; officers with less than three years are called "slick-sleeved rookies". Many officers refuse to sew on hash marks until they get three or four, which translates to nine or twelve years of service, well past the "seven year itch" when some officers quit.

There are three separate and distinct parts to the process of integration of a new employee. Champoux (2006) believes that part of the process begins even before the employee joins the organization; part happens once the employee joins, and part happens after the employee has worked there awhile.

The socialization is continuous throughout the life of the employee, until retirement. The process is most intense during transition between phases, and may repeat itself in its intensity, when the employee gets promoted or changes jobs, locations, or assignments.

The goals of the organizational socialization may be hidden, and there is discourse as to whether these goals should be disclosed. Anakwe & Greenhaus (1999) state that no empirical study has examined socialization effectiveness.

Organizational socialization is an important part of workplace survival, and survival in general, but it has not been studied sufficiently; ethical, moral, and social issues should be examined, and the process should be smoothed, since the employee has so much at stake.

# Performance Appraisals

Job performance is a commonly used, yet poorly defined concept in industrial and organizational psychology, the branch of psychology that deals with the workplace. It most commonly refers to whether a person performs their job well. Despite the confusion over how it should be exactly defined, performance is an extremely important criterion that relates to organizational outcomes and success. Campbell (1990) describes job performance as an individual level variable; performance is something that an individual does.

It is crucial to make sure that the appraisal is really measuring the intended objectives or behaviors. If not, the organization encourages the wrong kind of work behaviors and produces unintended and sometimes negative outcomes.

For instance, if the number of traffic citations issued is an item in performance appraisal of police officers, it encourages them to sit on a corner of a street and pull over as many violators as possible during heavy traffic hours. The true purpose of a police force, which is public safety, may become secondary to issuing a large number of tickets for many officers.

A tertiary unintended outcome is the snarling of traffic in that area. Campbell (1990) defines performance as behavior. It is something done by the worker. This concept differentiates outcomes from performance. Outcomes are the result of a worker's performance, but they are also the result of other influences.

There are more factors that determine outcomes than just an employee's behaviors and actions. Ticket and arrest production is often referred to as self-initiated activity or Police Officer productivity.

Campbell and Campbell (1988) state that productivity can be thought of as a comparison of the amount of effectiveness that results from a certain level of cost associated with that effectiveness. Effectiveness is the ratio of outputs to inputs- those inputs being effort, monetary costs, resources, and the outputs being the number of tickets written, which translates to income for the city, county, or state.

Federal Agents are not peace officers, and as such are forbidden to issue tickets or arrest for misdemeanors.

Campbell, Dunnette, Lawler, & Weick.(1970) note the difference between individual controlled action and outcomes. In police work, a favorable outcome is a certain level of revenue generated through the issuance of citations.

There is an equally important fulfillment of the social contract to protect the community from traffic violators. Revenue can be generated or not, depending on the behavior of the officers. When the employee performs this task well, citation issuance goes up. However, certain factors other than employees' behavior influence citations generated.      For example, tickets might slump due to economic conditions, changes in traffic patterns, construction bottlenecks, weather, and traffic calming techniques. In these conditions, employee performance can be adequate, yet citation stats can still be low.

The first is performance and the second is the effectiveness of that performance. These two can be decoupled because performance is not the same as effectiveness.

Often in police work the negative is accentuated more often than the positive in performance appraisals. Positive outcomes are used more infrequently than negative outcomes. Police managers tend to think so much about liability and backing themselves up, that they feel they need to document everything that occurs so that they can issue reprimands that will not be overturned in the event that an officer does something wrong.

Frequently, Police Officers use

the term "attaboys" to describe a performance recognition or commendation. Also, frequently, Police Officers use the term "oh shit" to describe a reprimand, coaching, counseling, or write-up. Police Officers use the expression "it takes 20 attaboys to erase one "oh shit".

This is the "what have you done for me lately" mentality of police managers. Officers perceive that the managers, who are fully aware that each and every time a Police Officer goes to work, that officer may be killed, maimed, sued, harangued by the management, criticized by the media, or sacrificed by the politicians, fail to commend adequately, and never fail to correct.

Many police employees are assessed according to their characteristic traits, such as personality, aptitudes, attitudes, skills, and abilities; these traits are not always directly related to job performance. Trait-based assessment lacks validity and thus frequently raises legal questions. Many police managers unfairly and improperly base evaluations on personality and attitude.

There is favoritism, nepotism, cronyism, and rascalism in this rating system. It is not uncommon for one member of a group or clique to be promoted, and then to supervise members of that clique. Since officers bid for shift in many departments, officers can align themselves to be assigned to work for a particular sergeant they are friendly with. In some departments that bid quarterly, an officer may bid to work for one quarter for an "easy rater" during the quarter that their annual evaluation falls under. Some officers bid to work for sergeants who have a propensity to write more performance recognitions and fewer counselings or reprimands.

## Work Contexts

A work context is the necessary information, including interaction with the worker, to provide the user support in the actual working situation. Work contexts in law enforcement are often restrictive. Some departments assign an officer to a specific zone, and the officer is not allowed to leave that zone.

If the zone is a residential zone, and the officer is proficient in RADAR enforcement or DUI enforcement, that officer is restricted to zonal enforcement activities that are not conducive to traffic enforcement, but that are more conducive to community oriented policing and community policing.

Conversely, if the officer that is more crime prevention oriented, and is assigned to a highway or high traffic business district, then the context is not suited to that officer. Supervisors who assign officers to zones that closely mirror their areas of interest makes maximum use of the work context most appropriate to that officer. Oldham & Cummings (1997) say to ensure the most creative work from employees, managers need to assess the creative potential of each person and then place those with high potential into work contexts that stimulate and nurture it.

A police car is a patrol officer's office. A police detective or sergeant may work in a traditional office. Kirsh (2001) says offices are niches we inhabit and construct.

Officers, detectives, and ranking officers build elaborate workspaces with badges of honor and merit, and many joke items and humorous cartoons that help them cope with the stressors of their jobs.

Oldham & Cummings (1997) state that when firms place people with high creative potential in contexts that offer complex job assignments, supportive and non-controlling supervision, and competitive co-workers, they reap the benefits of maximum employee creativity.

Organizations need both leaders and managers. Managers handle day-to-day operations, and see to the smooth running of the organization. Leaders provide the vision and the direction for the organization. A leader has followers; this is the primary distinction between a leader and a manager; a manager has subordinates.

Champoux (2006) believes that one of the basic differences between leaders and managers is that leaders provide the vision and expect managers to carry out the activities necessary to accomplish the vision. Leaders form and carry out mission statements, vision statements, and define organizational values.

# Leadership and Management in Law Enforcement

The Chief of Police in a Police Department is the highest ranking leader; the Police Major Assistant Chief or Deputy Chief is the highest ranking manager in the Police Department. The Executive Officer to the Chief of Police authors the Mission Statement, Vision Statement, and Organizational Values. It is the responsibility of the Office of the Chief of Police to author these documents. It is the responsibility of the Assistant Chief to make sure these documents were adhered to.

Managers have subordinates, Leaders have followers. Managers have an authoritarian style. Leaders have a charismatic style. One problem with managers is that some managers believe they are leaders; the problem with this type of manager is that most employees wouldn't follow these would-be "leaders" across the street.

One problem with leaders is micro-management; some leaders believe they are managers in addition to leaders, and wind up adding a cumbersome layer to the management that slows down the organization.

In a law enforcement agency, the Chief of Police, Sheriff, Warden, Director, or other CEO is a leader. The sight of this person in full uniform and regalia should inspire confidence and pride; the Assistant Chief, Deputy Chief, Colonel, Major, Undersheriff, Assistant Warden, and Assistant Warden are managers.

For the sake of clarity, the terms Chief and Assistant Chief will be used to be synonymous with the other leaders and managers listed above.

A good Chief does not have to know what each officer, manager, or shift supervisor is doing. A Chief who is concerned with the mundane happenings of each arrest or call for service is a micro-manager.

If someone who knows the Chief on a personal level and complains to the Chief about a Police Officer, a citation, or an arrest, the proper response is for the Chief to hand the investigation off to the Assistant Chief, who will ask the Major to refer this to the Division Commander, (a Captain) who will then assign it to the Lieutenant, who will refer it to the Officer's Sergeant.

The answer will then be routed back up this chain of command to the Assistant Chief, who would contact the complainant for the Chief. This actively removes the Chief from the process, which protects the Chief from complaints of favoritism, and insulates the Chief from a host of problems, from nepotism to retaliation.

A Chief who receives a complaint about an officer, a citation, or an arrest, who calls the officer in and asks for information, cuts out all the managers, and in doing so undermines them. The Officer, who would normally feel very comfortable talking to his Sergeant about the matter, now worries if he arrested or cited a friend or relative of the Chief.

In Florida, as in most states, if the Chief orders a friend or relative to un-arrested, a citation voided, or orders an investigation quashed, commits a felony or misdemeanor, depending on the circumstances. Sadly, this happens every day in every county of every state in the Union.

Leadership, Metasystems and Flocking

Treating a population of individuals, such as an organization, as a single organism, is a metasystem. A metasystem is the sum of the parts. The human body contains millions of cells, each with a specific function; the cells combine to make items, which combine to make systems.

An analogy might be the term ecosystem, which defines the combined physical and biological components of an environment, such as a marine ecosystem.

The body is made up of systems; the muscular, urinary, reproductive, digestive, endocrine, respiratory, skeletal, integumentary, nervous, and cardiovascular, combine to make up the organism.

If the medical words are replaced with words such as administration, human resources, physical plant, maintenance, janitorial, communications, sales, research and development, Management information systems, and so on, it is easy to see how one could use this example to describe an organization.

A police department is a metasystem; it is also a group of systems, like the human body. Patrol Division, Services Division, and Criminal Investigations Division all are systems and all are run by managers.

Convergence, flocking, or entanglement theory, explains how a flock of birds, school of fish, he swarm of insects, or herd of beasts moves together, changing directions or behavior, without overt communication.

Davidson (2005) mentioned that flocking can be reproduced using a computer model for the coordinated motion of groups (or flocks) of entities called "boids". In artificial intelligence, this is replicated by an algorithm which models flocking behavior in nature.

This can also describe the mood or an organization. Flocking is an actual phenomenon in nature and in the computer world, and it is postulated herein that it exists in humankind, and specifically in Police Agencies.

A Police Department "flocks" based on political change, changes in morale, or changes passed down via a chain of command. Sometimes if the members of the organization are displeased or depressed by political situations, labor union / city management discord, or other negative environmental changes, work slows down in a measurable way, such as a reduction in tickets or arrests.

Sometimes if members of the organization are displeased or angered by an event, such as an officer being killed or injured, work increases in a measurable way, such as an increase in filed interviews of members of a certain population, a member of which may have killed or injured an Officer, or DUI arrests following an Officer being killed or injured by a drunk driver.

It is up to a leader to adjust the timbre of the organization and adjust these flocking behaviors, if they manifest themselves in way injurious to the organization; it is up to a manager to ensure that rules and regulations are adhered to, and if not, to adjust the behavior of these officers using assertive, progressive discipline.

Leadership involves setting a direction or vision for a group, while management controls the resources. Both Leadership and Management are necessary. Some leaders are not good managers, and some managers are not good leaders.

Leadership without management can lead to unrealistic goal-setting. Management without leadership can lead to goals being set with members not caring if the goals are met. Leadership combined with management sets a goal and manages the resources to achieve it. The problem is that we too often do not see leadership combined with management, since leaders and managers do not often work together, since managers (often middle management) are usually subordinate to leaders (CEO), and CEO's too rarely see the managers as partners instead of subordinates.

Conflict is common among people, and it is common in organizations. Entire industries have evolved to deal with conflict – in marriage, among co-workers, between organizations, between nations.

Ambassadors and embassy staff thrive on conflict. The entire diplomatic service exists to capitalize on, and to assist with the conflicts that will inevitably ensue between peoples and nations. Conflict can be either functional or dysfunctional.

When dysfunctional conflict erupts in violence, the human and financial cost can be staggering. Rugala (2003), estimates the costs, from lost work time and wages, reduced productivity, medical costs, workers' compensation payments, and legal and security expenses, at many billions of dollars.

## Functions and Dysfunctions of Conflict

Conflict in the workplace is not only common, it is expected. Champoux (2006) defines conflict within the context of Industrial Organization Psychology, as doubt, questioning, opposition, or controversy. This is a wide ranging, general definition, but useful, in that it allows us to explore the idea of asynchronous communications, controversy, and disharmony in an organizational setting.

Jealousy, anger, sadness, internal variables, external variables, interoffice politics, racial tension, almost anything can be the genesis of conflict. The penultimate goal is to rise above conflict, and continue the business of business.

It is the job of the manager to assist and sometimes regulate, in order to align employees toward the goal of harmonious work, and it is the job of the leader to repair the feelings of consanguinity that once fueled the machine and machinations of the machine, prior to that conflict. Champoux (2006) states that conflict is basic and needs managing; it is possible to say that it needs leadership as well.

According to Rugala (2003), on August 20, 1986, a postal worker named Patrick H. Sherrill, facing possible dismissal after a troubled work history, walked into the Edmond,

Oklahoma, post office, where he worked and shot 14 people to death before killing himself.

In just the previous three years, four postal employees were killed by present or former coworkers in separate shootings in Johnston, South Carolina, Anniston, Alabama and Atlanta, Georgia. In August 1989, in a Los Angeles Times account of yet another post office shooting.

Disturbingly, we have seen in the last decade, a dramatic rise in the incidence of murder and murder-suicide at work, the most radical of dysfunctional conflict. The old joke about "going postal" has not been contained among postal workers.

Workplace violence is among the most important issues at the workplace and probably the most important in the area of dysfunctional conflict.

According to OSHA (2002), violence in the workplace is violence or the threat of violence against co-workers. It can occur at or outside the workplace and can range from threats and verbal abuse to physical assaults and homicide, one of the leading causes of job-related deaths.

When conflict erupts as workplace violence, Law Enforcement comes into play. Scanlon (2001) queries, who among us haven't asked the question, "what if it happens at my workplace, my auto parts plant, my job, my college or university?"

OSHA (2002) states, over two million American workers are victims of workplace violence each year. Workplace violence can strike at any time, on any shift, anywhere, and no one is immune. Among workers at increased risk are those who exchange money with customers; deliver passengers, goods, or services; or work alone or in small groups, during late night or early morning hours, in high-crime areas, or in community settings and homes where they have extensive contact with the public.

This group includes health-care and social service workers such as visiting nurses, psychiatric evaluators, psychiatrists, psychologists, mental health professionals, therapists, and probation officers; community workers such as electrical, gas and water and sewer utility employees, phone and cable TV installers, and; retail workers; taxi drivers, and of course, postal workers.

According to Rugala (2003), in Southern California alone, over an eight-year span from mid-1989 to mid-1997, there were 15 workplace homicide incidents, six with multiple victims, which killed a total of 29 people.

In subsequent years, conflict resulting in workplace violence erupted across the country, including four state lottery executives killed by a Connecticut lottery accountant (March 1998); seven coworkers killed by a Xerox technician in Honolulu (November 1999); seven slain by a software engineer at the Edgewater Technology Company in Wakefield, Massachusetts (December 2000); four killed by a 66-year-old former forklift driver at the Navistar Plant in Chicago (February 2001); three killed by an insurance executive at Empire Blue Cross and Blue Shield in New York City (September 2002); three killed by a plant worker at a manufacturing plant in Jefferson City, Missouri (July 2003); and six killed by a plant worker at a Lockheed-Martin aircraft plant in Meridian, Mississippi (July 8, 2003).

# Workplace Violence and Law Enforcement's Role in Workplace Conflict

The way Law Enforcement responds to these scenarios has changed radically. In the past, Police Officers would cordon off the area, and await SWAT, ERT, and hostage negotiators. Now, we see that time is of the essence, and that these are not "barricaded suspects" with a statement to read; these are killers who wish to kill as many co-workers or bosses as possible, before killing themselves – these are now known as "active shooter scenarios".

According to the El Paso County Sheriff's Office Policy and Procedure Manual (2004), An active shooter is defined as an armed person who has used deadly physical force on other persons and continues to do so while having unrestricted access to additional victims.

Scanlon (2001) states, the "active shooter" normally has an excellent tactical plan that involves randomly shooting as many people as possible, as quickly as possible, prior to committing suicide.

The only way Police Officers can minimize the number of casualties is to neutralize the shooter. If the Officers become pre-occupied with evacuating people, treating the injured, or searching the rooms, the shooter will be left free to maximize the body count.

The shooter must be challenged immediately, the surrender decision forced immediately, and only will the first responders be in a position to get medical assistance to those who need it.

In an active shooter scenario, the police are now trained to work together to make a dynamic entry using only the handguns they are issued, with an occasional AR-15 battle rifle in .223 caliber.

Many officers are now purchasing their own AR-15 rifles, and qualifying with them, so they may be authorized to carry them on patrol, for just this situation. Others are being issued these battle rifles by their departments.

In contrast, European police are issued larger, heavier caliber FN-FAL battle rifles in .308 caliber, or Heckler and Koch machine guns. Even the Pope's "Swiss Guard" and the famed guards at Buckingham Palace are issued FN-FAL battle rifles in .308 caliber, in contrast to our own American police, who usually carry only a handgun.

In a workplace violence scenario, the active shooter may be armed with rifles, shotguns, handguns, and even homemade bombs. This is why, according to the El Paso County Sheriff's Office Policy and Procedure Manual (2004), when an active shooter begins his attack, it is imperative that the initial police responders immediately pursue and establish contact with the shooter at the earliest opportunity.

Scanlon (2001) says that the sooner the shooter can be contained, captured or neutralized, the fewer the casualties incurred. During the action, Police Officers will move through unsecured areas, and bypass dead, injured, and frightened citizens while, approaching the subject or subjects.

It is important for law enforcement personnel to survive the encounter to end a massacre, rather than become additional victims; it is crucial to end the killing. This goes against the SWAT paradigm set up in 1968 by Chief Darryl Gates and the LAPD SWAT, the first such unit in the country, which mandated backing off and waiting for SWAT.

Gates (1992) relates that he originally named the platoon "Special Weapons Assault Team", but changed it to "Special Weapons And Tactics" for political reasons. Rather than wait for the "assault team", modern thinking is that even a lone officer with a handgun can be effective in thwarting an active shooter.

Borsch reports their reality research has established that aggressive action, by even a solo actor, has been, and is now, the most effective countermeasure in stopping the active killer.

Lloyd (2000) made the case for the need for "Immediate Action Rapid Deployment" (IARD) by police first responders, by stating that instead of being taught to wait for SWAT, Police Officers are receiving the training and weaponry to take immediate action during incidents that clearly involve active shooters' use of deadly force.

Scanlon (2001) notes that during the summer of 1999, a group of S.W.A.T. officers from the Columbus Ohio Division of Police developed a tactical plan that can be used, universally throughout law enforcement circles to deal with these horrendous situations. This plan known as the "QUAD" (QUick Action Deployment) concept was born.

On the investigative side, the Federal Bureau of Investigation takes workplace conflict seriously. According to Rugala (2003), The FBI's National Center for the Analysis of Violent Crime (NCAVC), part of the Critical Incident Response Group (CIRG), located at the FBI Academy at Quantico, Virginia, consists of FBI Special Agents and professional support staff who provide operational support in the areas of workplace violence counterterrorism, and threat assessment.

Typical cases received for services include child abduction, serial murder, serial rape, single homicides, multiple homicides, threats, and assessment of dangerousness in such matters as workplace violence, school violence, domestic violence, and stalking.

Conflict can be either functional or dysfunctional. Nearly all growth comes from conflict. The greatest advances in medicine, surgery, cartography, maritime navigation, mountaineering, strategy, and aviation have come to us as a result of wars, or threats of wars, the ultimate conflict.

Change is never comfortable or comforting. Most people fear and abhor change, and in turn fear the agents of change, often resulting in conflict. If as the hackneyed saying goes, necessity is the mother of invention, than conflict is the mother of necessity, and therefore the grandmother if invention.

Invention is the greatest of human achievement. The synthesis born of evaluation and analysis, invention is the penumbra of mankind, the zenith to give foil to the nadir that is war. War is the worst of man's waste of resources, life, and industry. It has been said that in the trenches of war, even the agnostic finds religion.

The most read book in the world is The Bible. The Biblical Book of the Revelation of John, usually referred to simply as Revelation, is the last book of the New Testament. Many who have read this have focused on the "apocalypse" (an unveiling of something unknown.) or "Armageddon", commonly referred to as the end of the world, but also meaning a "decisive or catastrophic conflict".

If "apocalypse" can be taken to mean "change", and "Armageddon" taken to mean "conflict", then even the agnostic can find symbolic meaning in the Bible, in that conflict leads to change.

Change may not always be positive, but it always leads to growth and synthesis. No one could argue against the statement that religion has been responsible for both conflict and change, be it Judaism, Christianity, Islam, Buddhism, or Zoroastrianism.

This functional and dysfunctional conflict has lead to many of the watershed events in the last 3000 years.

# Police Suicide

Violanti (2008) feels that due to stress, danger and availability of firearms, one might expect an increased risk of police suicide. Research statistics demonstrate that officers kill themselves more than they are killed by others. Violanti (2008) refers to epidemiological studies that show that the risk of police suicide is over three times that of the general population and risk has appeared to increase over the past decade.

It is appalling to think of the number of officers who take their own lives. Violanti (2008) says that the first step is to recognize that the problem exists. With regard to police suicide, police departments must take initiative, and realize that one police suicide is too many and agencies must be proactive in their attempt to prevent such events.

In it is likely that many police suicides are intentionally misclassified as accidents or undetermined deaths in order to protect suicide victims and survivors, and to protect insurance claims for the beneficiaries. Violanti (2008) mentions that suicide prevention efforts focus on identifying factors that can be changed, such as knowledge and identification of risk factors and attitudes towards seeking help with personal problems.

Violanti (2008) suggests an organizational model to include psychological assessment, training to help officers recognize and avoid psychological factors leading to suicide, stress awareness to include identification of stress, the value and techniques of physical exercise, benefits of proper nutrition, interpersonal communication methods, and coping styles, executive level training including organizational change and assistance with line officer problems, intervention, to facilitate officers in taking the first difficult step to intervention, and increasing accessibility to confidential psychological services, and. retirement counseling seminars to be made available to officers as early as five years prior to retirement.

# Part 2: Physical Preparation

It's never too late to be
who you might have
been.

~ George Eliot

# Firearms

Shooting is a skill that degrades over time. Officers should shoot their guns every month, and practice drawing from the holster weekly. This is not something that is debated.

Most officers shoot only once a year and never practice drawing. This is due to laziness. A civilian would think that an officer would want to practice with the arm that might save his life, but most cops simply don't practice.

There is a story that is very common in the police world. Ron (name changed) was a 34 year veteran. Ron probably should have retired years ago, but after the death of his wife, Ron simply had nothing else to do.

Ron never had any kids, due to an accident that happened when he was a kid. The 63 year old entered the police department after serving in the Marine Corps. Ron wasn't a drinker, but poured a bit of Irish whiskey into his glass every now and then. Ron didn't bowl, and had few hobbies. Ron figured a retirement would be boring. Most of Ron's friends had retired and died. Ron was found shot to death in a dark warehouse. Ron's revolver was in his right hand. The old police revolver probably should have been traded in for a semiautomatic pistol a decade earlier. Ron simply liked the old "wheelgun" and wanted to keep using it.

The crime scene investigator noted that the gun was frozen and the action could not be functioned. The CSI had to take the gun apart. The rounds in the gun were a semi-jacketed hollow point of a brand the department had gone away from over six years prior. The rounds had green verdigris on them.

It was determined that Gene, a 32 year veteran, and the Chief range Officer at the departmental shooting range had simply signed off on Ron for years. Ron probably had not fired that gun for a decade. Gene admitted that he and Ron would sit and drink coffee and swap stories when Ron came to the range every six months to qualify.

Ron's funeral was attended by thousands. Shopkeepers, housewives, and politician, students, firemen, and teachers lined up to file past the kindly old veteran's casket. Ron was a big man. At over six feet and nearly 275 pounds, Ron was a big muscular guy who had gone a little soft.

The department's brass spent hours eulogizing the old veteran, who was the last of his breed. They said he died valiantly with his gun in his hand. They never told the mourners that Ron's gun was as useless as a paperweight.

The day of the funeral, January 29th, Gene quietly retired and did his final paperwork at the nearly deserted city hall, while his friend was buried. Every year on January 29th, gene visits the grave and pours a bit of Irish whiskey on the mound to salute the old war horse.

Gene had a few good years left in him, drinking coffee and teaching slick sleeved rookies how to shoot, but he "pulled the pin" early and retired. He sits in front of the television, watching cop shows and reading gun magazines. Gene hasn't shot a gun since Ron's death. Ron had a few good years left in him too. Ron's death was needless, pointless, and a damn shame.

Many cops will spend hundreds of dollars on firearms, but refuse to spend their own money on training. Ammunition, range fees, and training tuition are cheap compared to the cost of hospitals and lost wages.

There are several good civilian firearms instructors out there, including Ken Hackathorn, Ed Gottlieb, James Bigwood, and Andy Stanford. There are big fancy outfits like Thunder ranch and Gunsite. Some instructors will run a 3 gun course, where officers can transition from an AR15 to a handgun, or from a handgun to a shotgun.

Schools on tactics, weapons choice, and marksmanship are available to civilians and officers alike.

The National Rifle Association can refer interested persons to police, security, and civilian courses all designed to hone skills.

This book isn't designed to be a how-to book on tactics or shooting, but one would be remiss not to mention the difference between cover and concealment. Concealment simply makes it harder for an assailant to see you. Bushes are concealment. A blue freestanding mailbox or car is cover.

Taking a good position behind an engine block is preferable to hiding. Having good equipment which is well maintained is essential.

# Off Duty Carry

This may be controversial, but I would never recommend a single action "cocked and locked" gun for anyone, law enforcement or otherwise, this day and age. This is neither the military nor the OK corral. I should mention that the military did away with the 1911 Government model.

Many good manufacturers are making and selling Cold Government clones: Strayer Tripp, Les Baer, Remington, Springfield Armory, Smith and Wesson, Sig Sauer, and Norinco, just to name some. They make great range guns, they are fun to shoot, and they are great sellers. They are accurate and dependable.

I offer this question: Tomorrow at 5:00 PM, you will get into a gunfight. You may bring anything you own. What will you bring? Some may answer that they would bring a Sig Sauer P226 in 9mm Nato with two spare magazines. Some may answer that they would bring a Glock 21 in .45

ACP with a flashlight and a spare magazine. Some may answer that they would bring a Glock 35 in .40 S/W caliber and a pair of handcuffs.

Some may answer that they would bring a Colt 1911 .45 tricked out by John Nowlin, 4 magazines, a Smith and Wesson M 640 Centennial .38 Special as a backup, and pack it all in a Sam Andrews Urban Safari rig.

My response to these choices is this: then do it! Why are you packing a Beretta .32 in a pocket holster or a Smith and Wesson M66 in an ankle holster, if this is not your first choice? You already know what you would carry if you were all ready to go serve a warrant, so why not carry that gun off duty?

Is it really easier to conceal a Glock 27 than it is to conceal a Glock 35? If you are carrying in a hip holster, they really aren't much different. Obviously, if you are carrying your Glock 27 in an ankle holster, there is a difference. In a shoulder holster, there really isn't.

When people complain and mention they can't wear a favorite jacket or shorts while concealing a big pistol, I spout this maxim:

*"Don't change your gun. Change your clothes."*

# The Training Star

The training star is a good device to illustrate the concept of synergy. The star represents the six tenets of the program, training, education, practice, hardware, skill, and policy.

Training is the center of the star. Law Enforcement Officers should never stop training. If a department is found to be deficient in its training of officers, in some cases, the liability transfers to the individual officer, for not requesting training, and in some cases to the supervisor, for not recommending training.

# Weissberg's First Law: Successful Survival

has six tenets:

**Tenet one:** If you survive the encounter, but are maimed, disfigured, or crippled, you have been unsuccessful.

**Tenet two:** If you survive the encounter, but have left yourself open to civil lawsuits, and are rendered penniless, you have been unsuccessful.

**Tenet three:** If you survive the encounter, but are fired or sent to prison, you have been unsuccessful.

**Tenet four:** If you survive the encounter, but are responsible for the death of another officer, or an innocent bystander, you have been unsuccessful.

**Tenet five:** If you do not survive the encounter you have been unsuccessful.

**Tenet six:** If you survive the encounter, but are ridden with guilt, emotionally crippled, or are rendered unstable, you have been unsuccessful.

**Goal:** If you survive the encounter, and come out mentally, physically, emotionally, financially, and legally, only then have you have been successful.

## Weissberg's Second Law: Career Termination:

Every Law Enforcement Officer (who does not quit), finds that his or her career ends with that officer retired, fired, or expired. Make sure that you end your career with the suffix "ret." After your name, and live to enjoy a long and successful retirement.

The keys to retirement are found in the training star. The training star has six tenets to the program: training, education, practice, hardware, skill, and policy. Note that this number repeats: **Weissberg's Second Law: Successful Survival** also has six tenets.

These tenets can be applied to the six areas of preparation presented in this book:

Part 1: Mental Preparation
Part 2: Physical Preparation
Part 3: Emotional Preparation
Part 4: Legal Preparation
Part 5: Financial Preparation
Part 6: Final Preparation

# Quick Reference
## The Training Star's Six Tenets

## Training

Training is an important issue, and rests in the center of the training star. In most badges, the state seal is in the center. The center of the authority lies with the state; the center of the officer lies in the training. An officer should seek training, seek new methodologies, and evaluate his or her own training constantly.

## Education

A truly modern officer has an education. A GED or high school diploma just will not do. Most departments offer tuition reimbursement. Some offer 100% tuition reimbursement.

This could add up to 10,000 worth of value to your salary and compensation package each year you are in school. Many departments figure that no one will take advantage of this benefit, so they do not limit this benefit. It is possible to get a department to pay for an associate's degree, bachelor's degree, master's degree, and even doctorate or law degree. Not taking advantage is like turning down free money.

The officer with a master's degree may find outside employment with a college, university, or police academy, and can earn up to $20,000 annually, without the risk and fatigue of working extra-duty jobs.

The college, university, or police academy may pay from 25 to 50% more than the off-duty job would pay, so the officer works less and makes more. The educated officer has less liability, and knows more. The educated officer has options in the event of job-related disability.

A bachelor's degree and master's degree can help with mental preparation, physical preparation, emotional preparation, legal preparation, financial preparation, and final preparation, in that many of these topics are covered in general curriculum.

## Practice

Training is worthless if the techniques are not practiced. Psychomotor master begins after a thousand repetitions. A thousand repetitions is equal to only 20 boxes of pistol ammunition. Since most departments requite only two boxes of ammunition fired annually, it would take a decade to reach the most basic level.

Even then, the skill is frangible and decays. It is said that a black belt signals that the student is ready to begin. Have you ever requested additional ammunition or training time? Have you ever requested inservice training on topics such as rapid action techniques, patrol carbine, or a tactical shooting course?

## Hardware

Hardware is your equipment. Your police car, duty leather, pistol, rifle, shotgun, knife, TASER, pepper spray, baton, radio, and boots all require daily inspection.

Your car or motorcycle should be deadlined immediately if any safety feature is inoperable. It is possible you will have to drive a "stinker" (a pool car) for awhile, and will have to unpack 200 pounds of gear from your car, and put it into the pool car. That is easier than having eight honor guards carry your 200 pounds up church steps in an ornate casket.

## Skill

There are many physical skills required for this job. Firearms, driving, defensive tactics, and verbal communication are all skills that we learn in basic academy, and most cops never retrain in those areas again. The fault is yours. Own the fault! If you have not requested training, you will not get it, unless you have demonstrated a deficiency that someone has noticed.

If you have demonstrated a lack of mental preparation, physical preparation, emotional preparation, legal preparation, financial preparation, or final preparation, chances are it may be too late.

**Policy**

You cannot make policy or change policy, unless you hold a specialized position in the department. You are responsible for knowing and following policy. The department demands it, the law demands it, and the supervisors demand it.

It is unrealistic and foolish to demand that a cop know 800 pages of policy, but they do demand that. The only reasonable response to that is to study and know your policy. The lynchpin of most sergeant's and lieutenant's exams is knowing departmental policy. At the very least, you should be familiar with the high liability policies.

# Martial Arts

If you cannot be a poet, be the poem.

~ David Carradine

Martial Arts and Martial Science are a wonderful way of life. Preparing for attack and defending using your body and objects of opportunity can save your life. There is simply no other way to say it. There are times, places, and locations where carrying a gun is simply not allowed or not feasible. Sometimes a knife is allowed. Sometimes a wooden walking cane is allowed. Sometimes only a sharpie marker stands between you and danger.

There is simply no excuse for being untrained. There are many schools of martial arts (sometimes called *dojos)* where cops can learn. The martial world is complex, but all arts are bio-mechanical. The arm only bends one way, and to try to bend it in a way it won't go will cause pain or destruction. The arm-bar is an example. The following is a review of some martial styles, and is in no way complete; one can use this as a starting point before beginning research.

# Terms

*Abaniko*: a fixed blade knife designed by GM Bram Frank.

*Balisong*: A Filipino adaptation of a Spanish sailor's knife that is sometimes called a "butterfly knife".

*Bushido*: three Japanese words which when combined mean "the way of the warrior-student".

*CRIMPT*: Close Range Medium Impact Tool, designed by GM Bram Frank.

*Dan:* a black belt level, as in 3$^{rd}$ Dan, 7$^{th}$ Dan, etc.

*Datu*: a Grandmaster in the Filipino Style.

*Desangut*: a kinetic opening knife designed by GM Bram Frank, based on a Filipino Kerambit knife.

*Dobok*: a martial arts uniform for Korean martial arts.

*Dojo*: a martial arts training room or hall.

*Dojo Kun*: a Japanese martial arts term meaning dojo rules.

*Drone*: a training knife made of metal.

*Escrima*: a rattan stick used for Filipino Arnis, Kali, or Escrima stick fighting and training.

*Gi*: a martial arts uniform for Japanese martial arts.

*Grandmaster*: usually a $7^{th}$ degree black belt or higher rank, in any style.

*Gunting*: a kinetic opening knife designed by Bram Frank.

*Guro*: a black belt in the Filipino Style.

*Cane-Fu:* A martial science based on the Filipino weapon, renamed by GM Joe Robaina.

*Kerambit*: a Filipino knife with a ring on one end.

*Ki:* Energy in Japanese (also Chi and Qui).

*Kohai:* junior in Japanese.

*Kubotan*: A short stick developed by developed by Takayuki "Tak" Kubota.

*Lapu-Lapu Corto*: a kinetic opening knife designed by Bram Frank.

*Master*: an instructor with a black belt, who may run his own school or style.

*Master of Tapi-Tapi*: a very high ranking grandmaster in Filipino Arnis.

*Presas Bolo*: a bolo machete for Filipino knife fighting, popularized by Professor Remy Amador Presas.

*Professor*: the acknowledged highest ranking instructor in a style. The professor may be the founder of a style, or may have inherited the title. A Professor normally has a $10^{th}$ degree black belt or higher (some styles have 11 or 12 ranks).

*Sempai:* Senior in Japanese.

*Sensei*: a teacher, in any style.

*Sifu*: a teacher, in any style.

*Takonoma*: an alcove for keeping swords or knives. A photo of a revered teacher or a statue of a Buddha or bodhisattva is sometimes kept here also, along with a flower arrangement or calligraphy scroll or painting.

*Trainer*: a training knife made of resin or metal.

*Tusok*: a kinetic opening knife designed by Bram Frank.

*Yawara:* A short stick.

# BUSHIDO

武士道

# SEVEN VIRTUES
# OF BUSHIDO

RECTITUDE (義 GI)

COURAGE (勇 YŪ)

BENEVOLENCE (仁 JIN)

RESPECT (礼 REI)

HONESTY (誠 MAKOTO)

HONOR (名誉 MEIYO)

LOYALTY (忠義 CHŪGI)

FILIAL PIETY (孝 KŌ)

WISDOM (智 CHI)

CARE FOR THE AGED (悌 TEI)

# THE EXCELLENT
# STYLES

I call these styles the "excellent styles" since they are excellent for police officers. Some styles have ground fighting or flying spinning kicks. I believe that an officer should never go to the ground wearing a full duty belt, and that flying spinning kicks are not for police officers, for legal and practical reasons.

## Filipino Arnis

Arnis may be known as Escrima, Eskrima, or Kali. This art is known by several other names as well. Modern Arnis is the system of Filipino martial arts founded by Professor Remy Amador Presas and brought to the United States and the world from the Philippines. The goal was to create an injury-free training method as well as an effective self-defense system in order to preserve the older Arnis systems.

Arnis relies on the Presas Bolo type machete, but also incorporates stick, knife, staff, cane, rope, empty hand, and other tools. This art is excellent for police, since most of us carry a stick (ASP, Monadonock, or other type), a pocket knife, and of course our hands. The primary weapon is the rattan stick, called a cane or baston (baton), which varies in size, but is usually about 28 inches; the ASP is available in a 26" size.

The death of Professor Presas left a void. Several family members including Ernesto Presas and Remy P. Presas. Several students claimed Professor Presas named them Punong Guro ("Head teacher"), Datu ("leader" or "Prince"), or "Master of Tapi-Tapi". There are many practitioners that can and will teach this beautiful and useful art.


Small Circle Ju Jitsu

Professor Wally Jay, a $10^{th}$ degree grandmaster, is still active well into his 90's. Wally Jay was a contemporary of Remy Presas. The Professor's art, which makes use of trapping and locking using compact motions, uses a concept called "the flow" which Presas espoused. The two traveled with George Dillman teaching and learning from each other. The Small Circle techniques work particularly well for law enforcement and look "good" to bystanders, using minimal movements and the appearance of small amounts of force to meet attack.

Ryūkyū Kempo Tomari-te, Tuite, Kyusho Jitsu, and Dillman Karate International

These arts, taught by George Dillman, are known for emphasis on light- touch pressure-point knock-outs. This style is complex, and is difficult to master. Dillman is famous for his association with Muhammad Ali and Bruce Lee. Dillman is a controversial figure, but no one can doubt he is a great teacher, a powerful fighter, and a winning competitor. The Dillman styles work very well for law enforcement, and also look benign on camera if videotaped by bystanders.


## Common Sense Self Defense Street Combat (CSSD/SC)

This style was created by Grandmaster Bram Frank, a student of Remy Presas, Wally Jay, and George Dillman. Bram Frank was trained in Chinese Wing Chun and later Arnis, and then went forward and began to train in edged weapons exclusively. Frank's seminars focus on using the blade for blocking, trapping, and cutting.

Frank's style purports to have the student "learn in 6, teach in 12" meaning that basic lessons can be learned in six hours. Of course, six and twelve years respectively is more appropriate for basic mastery in this or any style. Bram has been a student for over 40 years, and would readily agree that one seminar will not a master make.

The knives and tools Bram created, including the Abaniko, Tusok, Lapu-Lapu Corto (LLC), CRIMPT, Drone, Gunting, and Desangut, are some of the most inventive and ingenious tools out there, and are arguably the first new martial weapons created in over a century.

# THE WONDERFUL STYLES

These styles are wonderful for development of confidence, discipline, and harmony. While they are great arts, they may not be as applicable to the police world. It is really up to the individual to decide if these styles are applicable for police work.

American Boxing (USA)
Boxing (United Kingdom)
Boxe Francais (France)
Cane-Fu (USA)
Dumog (Philippines)
Fencing
Gracie Jiu-Jitsu (Brazil)
Hapkido (Korean)
Hung Gar (China)
Jeet Kun Do
Judo (Japan)
Jujitsu (Japan)
Kapap (Israel)
Karate
Kendo (Japan)

# THE WONDERFUL
# STYLES

Kenpo Karate
Kenjitsu (Japan)
Krav Maga (Israel)
Kuk Sool Won (Korean)
Kung Fu
La Savate (France)
MMA Fighting
Muay Thai Kickboxing
(Thailand)
Ninjutsu (Japanese)
Pencak Silat (Indonesia)
Shotokan Karate (Japan)
Sumo (Japan)
Systema (Russia)
Tae Kwon Do (Korea)
Tai Chi Chuan (China)
Tang Soo Do (Korea)
Wing Chun (China)
Wrestling (USA)
Wushu (China)

# FOR FURTHER STUDY

Advanced Pressure Point Fighting of Ryukyu Kempo: Dillman Theory for All Systems Point Fighting by George A. Dillman and Chris Thomas

Advanced Pressure Point Grappling by George A. Dillman

Conceptual Modern Arnis by Bram Frank

Dynamic Ju Jitsu by Professor Wally Jay

Go Rin No Sho (A Book of 5 Rings) by Miyamoto Musashi (Translation: William Scott Wilson)

Hagakure : The Book of the Samurai by Yamamoto Tsunetomo (Translation: William Scott Wilson)

<u>Kyusho-Jitsu: The Dillman Method of Pressure Point Fighting</u> by George A. Dillman and Chris Thomas
<u>Modern Arnis: Philippine Style of Stick Fighting</u> by Remy A. Presas and Anthony Jalandoni

<u>Modern Arnis: The Filipino Art of Stick Fighting</u> by Remy A. Presas

<u>Musashi</u> by Eiji Yoshikawa

<u>Pressure Point Karate Made Easy: A Guide to the Dillman Pressure Point Method for Beginners and Young Adults</u> by George Dillman

<u>Shogun</u> by James Clavell

<u>Small-Circle Jujitsu</u> by Wally Jay

<u>Taiko</u> by Eiji Yoshikawa (Translation: William Scott Wilson)

<u>The Firearm as a Martial Arts Weapon</u> by Michael Weissberg

The Life-Giving Sword: The Secret Teachings From the House of the Shogun by Yagyu Munenori (Translation: William Scott Wilson)

The Lone Samurai: The Life of Miyamoto Musashi by William Scott Wilson
The Practical Art of Eskrima by Remy A. Presas

The Unfettered Mind: Writings from a Zen Master to a Master Swordsman by Takuan Soho (Translation: William Scott Wilson)

Grandmaster Bram Frank teaching a knife defense
instructor seminar at the Hialeah Police Department
in Hialeah, Florida

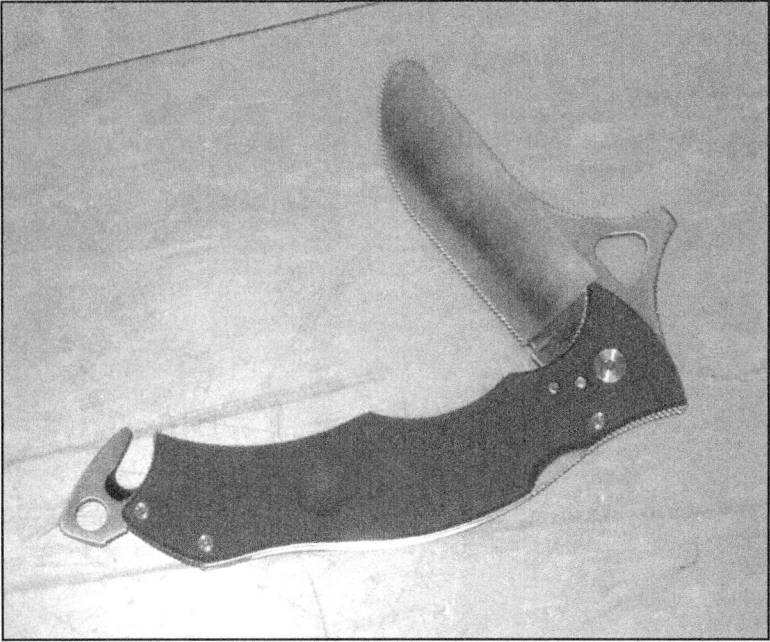

Grandmaster Bram Frank's CRIMPT, the Close
Range Medium Impact Tool. The first new martial
arts tool in over 100 years, designed for non-lethal
police use. This tool combines the teachings of
Remy Presas, Wally Jay, George Dillman, and
Bram Frank.

# Scenario: Call to assist elderly male acting strangely

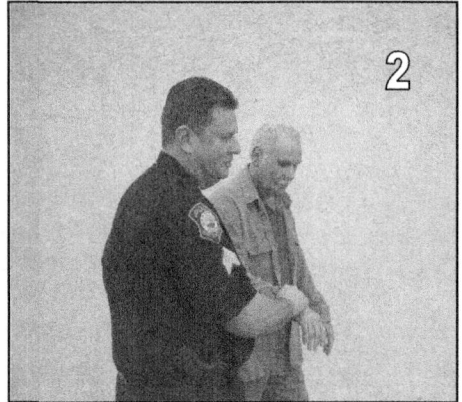

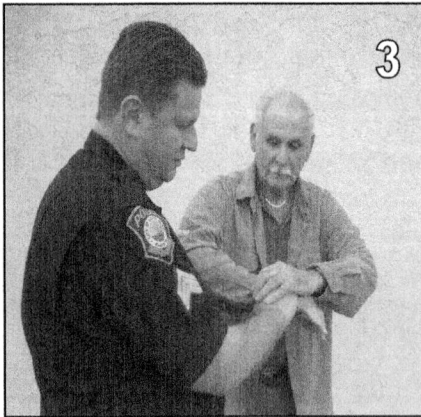

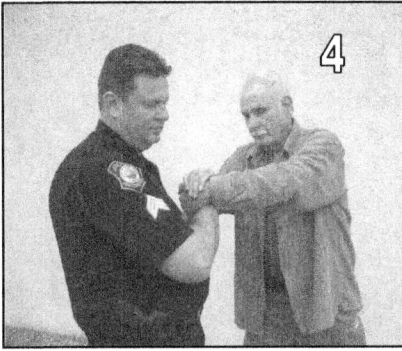

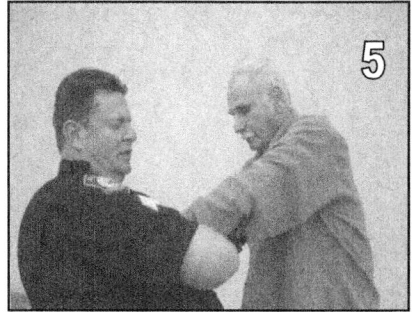

Lesson learned:  there is no such thing
as a harmless old man!

Rules violated:
Lack of concentration
Tombstone courage
Not heeding danger signs
Failure to watch the hands of a suspect
Relaxing too soon
Improper (no) handcuffing

Photo credit: Bram Frank

# Scenario 2: Call to assist elderly
## male acting strangely

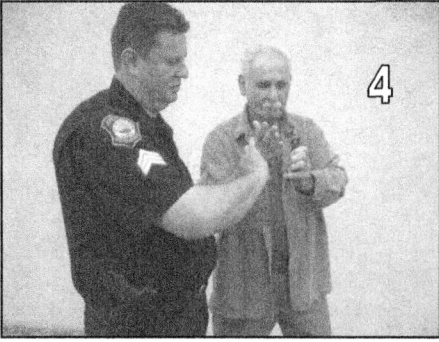

Lesson learned: there is no such thing
as a harmless old man when you are
dealing with 70 year old
Master Edward Gottleib!

Rules violated:
Lack of concentration
Tombstone courage
Not heeding danger signs
Failure to watch the hands of a suspect
Relaxing too soon
Improper (no) handcuffing
No search or poor search

Photo credit: GM Bram Frank

# Fitness for Duty

Getting ready for a career in law enforcement is tricky. I attended two police academies; The Federal Law Enforcement Training Center (FLETC) for the United States Border Patrol in Charleston, South Carolina, and the Basic Law Enforcement (BLE) academy at Miami Dade College, in Miami, Florida.

There was no guide to explain how to train to prepare for the academy. Yes, you must train before the academy.

It is not good enough to survive the four hours per day of physical exercise and torture. It is not good enough to survive the four hours per day of physical exercise and torture and stay awake for the four hours of lectures. It is not good enough to survive the four hours per day of physical exercise and torture and stay awake for the four hours of lectures and be able to pass every exam. It is not good enough to survive the four hours per day of physical exercise and torture and stay awake for the four hours of lectures and be able to pass every exam and be able to laundry every night and study.

At the FLETC we ran five miles per day in the swamps near the infamous Paris Island; we did over a thousand push-ups. We did nearly two thousand sit-ups. We were expected to do a half-dozen pull-ups.

How do you train to run five miles? By running eight miles. How do you train to do push-ups? By doing push-ups. How do you train to do sit-ups? By doing sit-ups. How do you train to do pull-ups? By doing pull-ups. There are no secrets here. The academy is a function of endurance.

Weight training, cycling, and swimming are fine, but they won't teach you to do push-ups, sit-ups, pull-ups, or to run. These four exercises will keep you fit for your job.

The good news (or bad news) is that ninety percent of the police agencies out there will never test you physically again. Your weight and fitness level never enter into your performance appraisals and there are cops with PCA (patrol-car ass) out there in every state in the Union.

In some of these old photos I look a bit chunky; I currently weigh 190 and bench press 225 at 6'01".

# Part 3: Emotional Preparation

Life is far too important a thing ever to talk seriously about.

~ Oscar Wilde

# Trauma

Trauma can happen at any time during a police officer's week. Traumatic episodes can include anything from a horrible traffic crash one is assigned to work, to beatings, rapes, murders, suicides and accidents.

An officer can recognize the victim as a family member, even if the person does not closely resemble the officer's family member; even the race or sex can be different. An officer can be seriously affected by any emotionally charged situation or tragedy.

Harming another person, though legal charges, self defense, or police involved shooting can traumatize an officer. Co-workers are slapping you on the back and "congratulating" you for killing another human being. In reality, the others are telling you they are glad you survived, and that they are glad they are not in your shoes.

Some officers will become angry, sad, withdrawn, or terrified after shooting, killing, or hurting another person. Remember, we are not the thugs with no conscience or morals or values – we are the cops who protect the weak from those people. Being "rough" has nothing to do with having no morals. The killing of another person is a terrible trauma.

The officer will not be encouraged to seek help. A good supervisor will demand the officer see someone in psych services, employee health, or in an employee assistance program. Even a police chaplain or spiritual advisor may help.

Try to remember to congratulate an officer who has just killed someone on their survival, and tell them you are glad they are still here. Do not congratulate them on killing.

## Personal Loss

Everyone has loss. Some examples are loss of money through a bad investment, loss of a girlfriend or boyfriend through a breakup, divorce, or the death of a parent or child.

We are not machines or robots. We act and react, and often don't realize the depth of our loss. It is a strange and visceral response that allows us to feel pain in the area of the heart, even though the actual realization of the loss happens in the brain. We can actually feel a "broken heart".

While most know that the heart is nothing but a pump, some actually feel acute loss as a chest pain. Grief is something we never really get over, but it gets better with time. The aggrieved knows this, but telling them or remind them is useless and will anger them.

# The Five Stages of Grief

The Kübler-Ross model, commonly known as the five stages of grief, was first introduced by Elisabeth Kübler-Ross in her 1969 book, On Death and Dying.

1. Denial—"I feel fine."; "This can't be happening, not to me." Denial is usually only a temporary defense for the individual. This feeling is generally replaced with heightened awareness of positions and individuals that will be left behind after death.

2. Anger—"Why me? It's not fair!"; "How can this happen to me?"; "Who is to blame?" Once in the second stage, the individual recognizes that denial cannot continue.
Because of anger, the person is very difficult to care for due to misplaced feelings of rage and envy. Any individual that symbolizes life or energy is subject to projected resentment and jealousy.

3. Bargaining—"Just let me live to see my children graduate."; "I'll do anything for a few more years."; "I will give my life savings if..."    The third stage involves the hope that the individual can somehow postpone or delay death. Usually, the negotiation for an extended life is made with a higher power in exchange for a reformed lifestyle. Psychologically, the individual is saying, "I understand I will die, but if I could just have more time..."

4. Depression—"I'm so sad, why bother with anything?"; "I'm going to die... What's the point?"; "I miss my loved one, why go on?"
    During the fourth stage, the dying person begins to understand the certainty of death. Because of this, the individual may become silent, refuse visitors and spend much of the time crying and grieving.
    This process allows the dying person to disconnect oneself from

things of love and affection. It is not recommended to attempt to cheer up an individual who is in this stage. It is an important time for grieving that must be processed.

5. Acceptance—"It's going to be okay."; "I can't fight it, I may as well prepare for it." In this last stage, the individual begins to come to terms with his mortality or that of his loved one.

The funeral helps the family progress through the grief stages. The pomp and circumstance of the police funeral allows the mourning of different persons – community members, partners, friends, and family. The police funeral allows for private moments, as well as public spectacle.

When one of our sentinels is murdered, it upsets our society's sense of order. The police keep us safe; when someone kills a police officer, this offends the society, and rips the fabric of our community.

## Mental and Emotional Fitness Training

Officers are trained in the use of firearms, batons, TASERS, pepper spray, cars, martial arts, and other survival and physical training, which is ongoing, as a result of the FDLE Mandatory Retraining Program, but Mental and Emotional Fitness Training, to include stress management, counseling, and responsible, emotional release, and the management of alcohol and drugs, is non-existent. Mental and Emotional problems, inability to manage stress, the need for counseling, inappropriate emotional release, and the use or abuse of alcohol and drugs, all are cause for de-certification, termination or desk duty, (the so-called "rubber gun squad").

It is hereby proposed that a mandatory Mental and Emotional Fitness Training Program be instituted, to include stress management, counseling for all officers, so that those who really need it are not singled out or ostracized, and that the stigma of requesting counseling for mental and emotional problems, inability to manage stress, the need for counseling, inappropriate emotional release, and the use or abuse of alcohol and drugs not be the cause for the end of a career, which in turn causes officers who need such help to avoid it like a plague.

Drunkenness is simply
voluntary insanity.

~ Seneca Indian Saying

# Alcoholism and Drug Addiction

Alcohol is found commonly in three forms; methanol, ethanol, and Isopropanol. Ethanol is grain alcohol, and is used in making drinking alcohol. Alcohol is a central nervous system depressant.

According to the DCEP program certified by the IACP, there are seven categories of drugs, including central nervous system depressants, central nervous system stimulants, hallucinogens, Dissociative anesthetics, narcotic analgesics, inhalants, and cannabis.

Central Nervous System Depressants slow down the operations of the brain and the body. Examples of CNS Depressants include alcohol, barbiturates, anti-anxiety tranquilizers such as Valium, Librium, Xanax, Prozac, and Thorazine), Gamma Hydroxybutyrate, Rohypnol and many other anti-depressants such as Zoloft and Paxil. Over 200 million prescriptions a year are written for Xanax alone.

CNS Stimulants accelerate the heart rate and elevate the blood pressure and "speed-up" or stimulate the body. Examples of CNS Stimulants include Cocaine, "Crack", Amphetamines and Methamphetamine.

Hallucinogens cause the user to perceive things differently than they actually are. Examples include LSD, Peyote, Psilocybin and Methylenedioxymethamphetamine (Ecstasy).

Dissociative Anesthetics include drugs that inhibit pain by cutting off or dissociating the brain's perception of the pain. PCP and it's analogs are examples of Dissociative Anesthetics.

Narcotic Analgesics relieve pain, induces euphoria and creates mood changes in the user. Examples of narcotic analgesics include Opium, Codeine, Heroin, Demerol, Darvon, Morphine, Methadone, Vicodin and Oxycontin.

Inhalants include a wide variety of breathable substances that produce mind-altering results and effects. Examples of inhalants include Toluene, plastic cement, paint, gasoline, paint thinners, hair sprays and various anesthetic gases.

Cannabis is the scientific name for marijuana. The active ingredient in cannabis is delta-9 tetrahydrocannabinol, or THC. This category includes cannabinoids and synthetics like Marinol and Dronabinol.

These seven categories of drugs affect the systems of the body, which are the muscular, urinary, respiratory, digestive, endocrine, reproductive, skeletal, integumentary, nervous, and circulatory.

Reporting for work after having used any of these substances within eight hours in inexcusable, and can result in termination. Using any substance that is a controlled substance without a valid prescription can and probably will result in termination and decertification if you are caught.

Seeking help for drug or alcohol addition may save your career and your life.

# Fidelity

Infidelity is the curse of the police officer. Many police officers have to work extra duty jobs to pay alimony and child support. Divorce is costly and unnecessary repercussion of infidelity.

Yes, it is true your wife or girlfriend will not understand this job. Yes, it is true your wife or girlfriend will not sympathize when you are ordered to hold over. It is true your wife or girlfriend will give you a ration of hell if you miss the anniversary dinner because you could not get the night off.

It is a guarantee, however, that it is true your wife or girlfriend will not forgive your hooking up with a cop groupie or a "hugger" because you are misunderstood.

Yes, it is true your husband or boyfriend will not like you riding with a male partner. It is true your husband or boyfriend will not like you being "one of the guys".

Now that we got that business out of the way, try to remember the times your husband or boyfriend or your wife or girlfriend stood by you, the times they supported you in the academy, the times they stood with you when you got a special award or commendation. Cheating will cost you in ways you cannot even imagine.

Seek the help of a spiritual advisor or chaplain, or a licensed counselor. Try not to let this job ruin your life and your marriage or relationship. Do not let this job destroy your relationship with your kids.

If everything else fails, go get a lawyer and find out how to get a divorce before you cheat. The experience of visiting the lawyer may convince you that it is worth one more try. It is way too easy to make a date with a "hugger" than it is to make an appointment with an attorney.

# Part 4: Legal Preparation

The power of the lawyer is
in the uncertainty of the
law.


~ Jeremy Bentham

# IAB
# Internal Affairs Bureau

The PBA states that the "Garrity" statement should be written as the first sentences on any statement, report, or memorandum an officer is ordered to write when the officer knows or has a reasonable belief that discipline may result.

This is the Garrity Statement: "It is my understanding that this report is made for administrative, internal police department purposes only. This report is made by me after being ordered to do so by lawful supervisory officers. I have not been permitted a reasonable amount of time to confer with a PBA representative or attorney. It is my understanding that by refusing to obey an order to write this immediately, that I can be disciplined for insubordination and that the punishment for insubordination can be up to, and including, termination of employment. This report is made only pursuant to such orders and the potential punishment/discipline that can result for failure to obey that order." The Garrity Rule stems from the court case Garrity v. New Jersey, 385 U.S. 493 (1967), which was decided in 1966 by the United States Supreme Court. Only in this profession can an employee be force to give a written account without the benefit of counsel – this is appalling, and the very essence of stress.

There is a well-known acronym in the intelligence community for the reasons for treasonous, unethical, or illegal behavior: MICE – money, ideology, conscience (or lack thereof), and ego. If one of the four conditions exist, the subject is likely to commit an unethical or treasonous act. Unethical behavior is born of greed, and guilt is assuaged by rationalization.

Emile Durkheim, introduced the concept of anomie in his book "The Division of Labor in Society", in 1893. He used "anomie" to describe a condition of deregulation or normlessness that was occurring in society; rules on conduct were breaking down and people did not know what to expect from each other.

Anomie, is a state where norms are ignored, confused, unclear, or not present. Norms are crucial in business; if a company or person cannot be trusted, then no one will do business with them. Business is more than just commerce, or the quest for lucre. Business is a language and society as real as any other.

## Violations of Policy
## (Pursuits)

IACP states that 61% of pursuits were initiated due to traffic violations or misdemeanors. This is interesting, since many departments allow pursuits only for forcible felonies. Failure to follow policy, resulting in a crash which kills or maims, is a career-ender, plus, civil penalties or criminal penalties may attach.

Lt. James `Jamie` Hurst Sears, 38, of Colonial Heights, died, Saturday, August 12, 2006. Sears was promoted to Lieutenant and was killed before he had a chance to wear his new rank.

Lt. Sears of the Colonial Heights, Virginia, Police Department was fatally injured in a collision in Chesterfield County. Sears' vehicle was hit head-on early on the morning of August 12, 2006, by a Chesterfield County police officer who was engaged in a high-speed chase at the time. Sears died in the hospital less than an hour later. He was the father of three young children.

The police officer who accidentally killed Sears was allegedly travelling at 110 miles per hour when he ran a light and hit Sears' vehicle head-on. The object of the pursuit was a stolen van allegedly driven by a career criminal, who later crashed the van into a utility pole two miles further on, but fled on foot.

The Supreme Court of Virginia denied an appeal by the man after his conviction for manslaughter in the death of Lt. Sears. In May 2008, Colonial Heights Circuit Judge Herbert C. Gill Jr. sentenced the man to a total of 20 years in prison, half the maximum sentence, which was what Commonwealth's Attorney sought.

In his appeal to the Supreme Court, the felon argued "that his actions did not directly cause Sears' death, but that Sears died solely because of the officer's decision to continue the high-speed chase into a populated area".

Chesterfield Patrolman Haywood E. James II, must live with the knowledge that he caught Douglas Michael Brown Jr., but that his actions resulted in the death of Lt. Sears. This officer was doing the right thing at the right time for the right reason, but in the wrong way. The officer unfortunately exceeded the limits of his ability and had tunnel vision.

Oklahoma County Sheriff John Whetsel, the past President of the International Association of Chiefs of Police knows the tragedy and pain caused by a bad pursuit. In 1980 his wife and 2-year-old daughter were killed during a police pursuit.

Sheriff Whetsel responded to the scene and at first did not recognize the burned hulk which split in two and erupted in flame, as his wife's car. When an officer ran a stop sign in Oklahoma City and hit the family car broadside.

The Sheriff was unaware of the identity of the victims; Whetsel was dispatched to the scene, where in addition to the two deaths, his 4-year-old daughter was critically injured. Since 1992, after a suggestion from Whetsel, officers are required to undergo specialized drivers training.

This tragedy happened when an Oklahoma Highway Patrol trooper pursued a speeding motorcyclist. When he figured out that it was his wife and daughter who had just been killed, Whetsel lunged, screaming, toward the smoking wreck; he was determined to get under the car. The distraught Sheriff was restrained by other officers.

Many Departments Are Starting To Think It's Not Worth Risking An Automobile Crash Over A Minor Traffic Violation. Chiefs are restricting when officers can participate in pursuits or chases. The U.S. Supreme Court is scheduled to hear a case that may clarify when a police officer can be sued over a deadly chase. The IACP has put out a model policy for departments.

## Case Law

It is absolutely impossible to be up to date on case law in a book like this, however, officers must know about several landmark cases that are precedents for any actions coming to court.

# Sacramento v. Lewis, 523 U.S. 833 (1998)

Sacramento v. Lewis, 523 U.S. 833 (1998) a decision of the Supreme Court of the United States involving police action in a high-speed car chase.

This case concerned a pursuit conducted by Sacramento County sheriff's deputies and two men on a motorcycle. Brian Willard was riding the cycle and Phillip Lewis was a passenger.

The motorcycle was weaving in and out of traffic at up to 100 miles an hour, and ended when Willard lost control and the bike crashed. One of the deputies could not stop in time and hit Lewis, killing him.

Lewis' parents sued the Sheriff's Department, accusing the deputy of depriving Lewis of his Fourteenth Amendment due process right to life through deliberate and reckless conduct. A district court ruled in favor of the deputy, the Ninth Circuit appeals court reversed, and then the

Supreme Court ruled unanimously in the department's favor.

The question before the Court was "does a police officer violate substantive due process by causing death through reckless indifference to life in a high-speed chase aimed at apprehending a suspected offender?" The answer was a unanimous "no." This decision brought us the "shocks your conscience" test.

Even though the blame for the killing rests with Willard, one would be ill advised to chase a speeding motorcyclist, especially since airships are so common in the United States. Letting an offender go even though the subject did not show respect for your authority may injure our pride, but this will not end your life or career.

Brower v. County of Inyo,
489 U.S. 593 (1989)

In this US Supreme Court case, Brower was killed when the stolen car he had been driving at high speeds to elude pursuing police crashed into a police roadblock. Survivors brought suit under 42 U.S.C. § 1983 in Federal District Court, claiming that police acting under color of law, violated Brower's Fourth Amendment rights by effecting an unreasonable seizure using excessive force.

The complaint alleged that police placed an 18-wheel truck completely across the highway in the path of Brower's car, behind a curve, with a police cruiser's headlights aimed in such fashion as to blind Brower on his approach. It also alleges that the fatal collision was a "proximate result" of this police conduct.

Anyone would think that this was irresponsible conduct. According to Pipes (2001), the U.S. Supreme Court ruled in favor of Brower, which led many police agencies to restrict the use of roadblocks to stop fleeing vehicles.


Tennessee v. Garner,
471 U.S. 1 (1985)

In Tennessee v. Garner, 471 U.S. 1 (1985), all Members of the Court agreed that a police officer's fatal shooting of a fleeing suspect constituted a Fourth Amendment "seizure."

The Supreme Court of the United States held that under the Fourth Amendment, when a police officer is pursuing a fleeing suspect, he or she may use deadly force only to prevent escape if the officer has probable cause to believe that the suspect poses a significant threat of death or serious physical injury to the officer or others.

October 3, 1974, Memphis Police Department Officers Wright and Hymon were dispatched to answer a burglary call.
Officer Hymon witnessed someone running across the yard. The fleeing suspect, Edward Garner, stopped at a chain-link fence.

Using his flashlight, Hymon could see Garner's hands, and was reasonably sure that Garner was unarmed. After Hymon ordered Garner to halt, Garner began to climb the fence. Believing that Garner would flee if he made it over the fence, Hymon shot him.

The bullet struck Garner in the back of the head, and he died shortly after an ambulance took him to a nearby hospital. Ten dollars and a purse taken from the burglarized house were found on his body.

Officer Hymon acted according to Tennessee state statute and Memphis Police Department policy authorizing deadly force against a fleeing suspect. The statute provided that "if, after notice of the intention to arrest the defendant, he either flee or forcibly resist, the officer may use all the necessary means to affect the arrest."

The question of whether Tennessee statute under authority of which the police officer fired the fatal shot was ruled unconstitutional as it authorized use of deadly force against apparently unarmed, fleeing suspect.

# City of Canton, Ohio v. Harris, 109 S. Ct. 1197 (1989).

In April of 1978, arrestee Geraldine Harris fell down several times, was incoherent following her arrest, and vomited blood, the officers summoned no medical assistance for her. After her release, she was diagnosed as suffering from several emotional ailments requiring hospitalization and subsequent outpatient treatment.

Harris filed suit seeking to hold the city liable under 42 U.S.C. § 1983 for its violation of her right, under the Due Process Clause of the Fourteenth Amendment, to receive necessary medical attention while in police custody.

The jury ruled in Harris' favor on thee claim on the basis of a city regulation that gave shift commanders sole discretion to determine whether a detainee required medical care, and suggesting that commanders were not provided with any special training to make a determination as to when to summon such care for an injured detainee.

It is bad policy and cruelty to not summon medical help for a prisoner in your care. The police are not here to punish, only to bring suspects before the court. Even if a subject is rude or nasty, it is good policy to summon medical help anytime a subject wants it.

Scott v. Harris, 550 U.S. 372 (2007)

Scott v. Harris, 550 U.S. 372 (2007) was a decision by the United States Supreme Court involving a lawsuit against a sheriff's deputy brought by a motorist who was paralyzed after the officer ran his eluding vehicle off the road during a high-speed car chase.

The driver stated that this action was an unreasonable seizure under the Fourth Amendment. The case also involved the question of whether a police officer's qualified immunity shielded him from suit under Section 1983.

The court sided with police and ruled that a "police officer's attempt to terminate a dangerous high-speed car chase that threatens the lives of innocent bystanders does not violate the Fourth Amendment, even when it places the fleeing motorist at risk of serious injury or death. "

The court did not address the fact that ramming a car with a push bumper at 91 miles per hour is not the definition of a PIT maneuver, and was probably not wise. The supervisor is heard saying on the tape "take him out, take him out".

## Bivens v. Six Unknown Named Agents, 403 U.S. 388 (1971)

Bivens v. Six Unknown Federal Narcotics Agents, 403 U.S. 388 (1971), was a case in which the United States Supreme Court ruled that an individual whose Fourth Amendment freedom from unreasonable search and seizures had been violated by federal agents.

Drug Enforcement Administration agents searched the house of the plaintiff, Webster Bivens, and arrested him without a warrant. Drug charges were filed but later dismissed by a U.S. Magistrate Judge. Bivens filed a lawsuit alleging the violation of his Fourth Amendment freedom from unreasonable search and seizure.

Without Bivens Actions, the right to hold Federal employees personally liable for malicious, vicious and even depraved actions is severely limited under the Civil Rights Act of 1964 and subsequent revisions.

## Civil Rights Act of 1871
## 42 U.S.C. § 1983

Section 1983 essentially made equitable relief available to those whose constitutional rights had been violated by an actor acting under State authority.

# DUI
## Driving Under the Influence

According to MADD, DUI kills over 30,000 people every year. Depending on the prior record and the specific nature of the case, these are just some of the D.U.I. penalties: the loss of the driver's license, fines, jail sentence, seizure of the vehicle probation and community service, increased automobile insurance rates or denial of insurance coverage for up to 10 years, a misdemeanor or felony conviction, mandatory alcohol education classes, installation of an ignition interlock system on the car, civil liability for any bodily injury or property damage caused, and a possible manslaughter, murder or homicide conviction.

A police officer with a DUI conviction is useless in court. The police are supposed to know better. It goes without saying, but police officers are human. You may go out and become intoxicated. A police officer will not be able to count on "badging your way out" of a DUI. A DUI will cost you your job, and it should cost you your job. Have someone else drive or take a cab. A DUI will cost anywhere from $8,000 to $20,000 to defend. It is cheaper to spend the $50 to take a cab if necessary.

The Mallenby effect is the phenomenon whereby self-perceptions of the effects of alcohol on the person change between the absorption and the elimination phases of alcohol consumption. During the absorption phase, individuals compare their perceived state with their condition before consuming alcohol. They tend to over estimate the effects of alcohol. During the elimination phase, they tend to underestimate their state of alcohol impairment.

What this means is that you may be incapable of deciding if you have had too much alcohol. Do not take the chance, take the taxi.

# Part 5: Financial Preparation

A penny saved, is a penny earned.

~ Benjamin Franklin

# Beginning your Career

Experts claim that as of this writing, you will need up to two million dollars for your retirement. This is because life expectancy is rising, as is the cost of living.

All in the Family

Remember All in the Family? The show was originally broadcast on the CBS television network from January 12, 1971 to April 8, 1979. In September 1979, the show was revamped, and given a new title, "Archie Bunker's Place". This version of the sitcom lasted another four years, ending its run in 1983.

Archie Bunker, the main character, was a dock worker and a cabdriver, and later a bar owner in the 1960's. Archie was able to work while his wife Edith stayed home.

They were able to feed, clothe, and educate their daughter Gloria, on a single income.  Archie and Edith later supported their daughter Gloria and their son-in-law Mike, and help to pay for their grandson Joey. Archie and Edith were only unusual in that an average family contained two children.

Most workers were able to rely on a pension, and so work 25 years and then enjoy a quiet retirement of 20-30 years before their deaths.  This is not the case these days.

The average cop dies within 5 years of retirement, due to stress, ill health, and poor preparation for the loss of the lifestyle of being a cop. This cop may be divorced, and may live alone.

If you intend to be an atypical cop, you may seek to retire at 55 with a spouse, and maybe have some children or grandchildren.  You currently may be married, and if so, may find it impossible to live Archie's modest lifestyle, even on two incomes.

It is suggested that you adopt of two strategies: either work extra-duty details or a second job, and put all of that money away for retirement or that you work your one job and put aside at least 25% of what you earn after taxes, for retirement. And that is with a defined pension plan in place.

The reason being is that the defined pension plan may not be in place when you retire, and the likelihood is that if it is, it will not be in the same form as it is today. There is also the great likelihood that Social Security might be modified or gone by then as well.

Your financial planner, lawyer, accountant, and investment banker should be able to assist you in evaluating what savings plans you should prepare to retire in a style you would like. A lawyer should be consulted before any life change, especially a marriage or divorce; a will should be updated upon any life change, such as marriage or the birth of a child.

There is a strong temptation to buy a new car, boat, nice jewelry, or spend lavishly. Resist the temptation.

The only good investment in one in yourself or your family's future.

# Investments Retirement Planning

Consult your financial planner, lawyer, accountant, and investment banker to assist you in evaluating what savings plans are best for you. The following information is to give you enough data so that you can ask the appropriate questions of your financial planner, lawyer, accountant, and investment banker.

Savings Account

The traditional savings account is no longer a good idea for retirement, only because the interest rate is so low. At the time of this writing, the rate of return is less than 1%, while the cost of inflation is over 4%. This means money left in a savings account loses value faster than it can make it up.

# IRA

An IRA is an Individual Retirement Account. An IRA is a personal savings plan that provides income tax advantages to individuals saving money for retirement purposes.

You invest money in an IRA, up to the amounts allowable under the tax law. These investments are called "contributions." In some instances an income tax deduction is available for the tax year for which the funds are contributed. The contributions, as well as the earnings and gains from these contributions, accumulate tax-free until you withdraw the money from the account.

You therefore enjoy the ability to generate additional earnings, protected from taxes on these earnings, each year the funds remain within the IRA. The IRA earns interest on the principal and the interest, which is called the "law of compounding interest".

The withdrawals of the funds from the IRA are termed

"distributions." Distributions are subject to income taxation, generally in the year in which you receive them.

Since the original purpose of the IRA is to assist you in providing for your own retirement, there is a penalty for withdrawing your IRA funds prior to an assumed retirement age of 59 1/2. This penalty is in the amount of 10 % of the distributions received by you prior to age 59 1/2, unless certain exceptions apply.

Sometimes the penalty can be avoided with proper planning. These distributions, whether before age 59 1/2 or later, are subject to income taxation upon receipt

You usually need to begin taking money from your IRA no later than April 1 of the calendar year following the date you attained age 70 1/2. The rules established by the government regarding these Required Minimum Distributions, their timing, the amounts, the recalculations, and the effect various beneficiary designations have on them, are among the most complex of the Internal Revenue Code. The penalty is 50 % of the shortfall between what you should have withdrawn and the amounts you actually withdrew by the proper date.

Traditional IRA

You can contribute up to $5,000 per year into an IRA. The amount of this contribution that is deductible on your income tax return depends on your Adjusted Gross Income and whether you are covered under an employer sponsored qualified retirement plan. Depending on your filing status your AGI, your contributions may range from fully deductible to totally non-deductible.

Education IRA

You can put away up to $500 per year into an education IRA, the money grows tax-free and has preferential tax treatment upon distribution to the beneficiary who uses it for authorized education expenses.

Roth IRA

Contributions are not deductible when the funds are contributed, but the Roth IRA earnings accumulate tax-free and remain tax-free upon distribution. This plan allows you to plan for your retirement without taxes.

Catch-Up Contributions

"Catch-up" contributions are for people aged 50 and over, in order to balance out the advantages of increased contributions for younger individuals. To be eligible for a catch-up contribution, an individual must first make the maximum regular contribution to his or her IRA or employer-sponsored plan. The maximum catch up contribution is $1000 per year.

401(k), 403(b), and 457 Plans

These are pretax contributions to certain employer- sponsored retirement plans. Remember that employers have the option of imposing lower limits than the government maximums, which is currently $15,000. If your employer matches finds in these accounts, and you do not take advantage, it is like turning down free money.

Annuities

An annuity is a contract between you and an insurance company, under which you make a lump-sum payment or series of payments. In return, the insurer agrees to make periodic payments to you beginning immediately or at some future date.

Annuities typically offer tax-deferred growth of earnings and may include a death benefit that will pay your beneficiary a guaranteed minimum amount, such as your total purchase payments. The minimum to invest is generally $10,000, but may be more or less. There are generally two types of annuities, fixed and variable.

## Certificate of Deposit

A CD is a special type of deposit account with a bank or thrift institution that typically offers a higher rate of interest than a regular savings account. Unlike other investments, CDs feature federal deposit insurance.

When you purchase a CD, you invest a fixed sum of money for fixed period of time and in exchange, the issuing bank pays you interest, typically at regular intervals. When you cash in or redeem your CD, you receive the money you originally invested plus any accrued interest. If you redeem your CD before it matures, you may have to pay an "early withdrawal" penalty or forfeit a portion of the interest you earned.

# Tips from the SEC

The Sec (Securities and Exchange Commission) has a webpage that offers investors tips. The webpage is http://www.sec.gov/index.htm. The SEC offers these tips:

Save and invest. Don't underestimate your ability to save and invest. With compound interest, even modest investments now can grow over time.

Lighten your credit load. Paying off high-interest debt may be your best investment strategy. Few investments pay off as well, or with less risk than, eliminating high-interest debt on credit cards or other loans.

Boost your "rainy-day" fund. Many experts recommend keeping about six months of expenses in a federally insured account to cover sudden unemployment or other emergencies.

"Sure thing" is fine as an expression but not as an investment pitch. Promises of guaranteed high returns, with little or no risk, are a classic warning sign of fraud. The potential for greater returns typically comes with greater risk. You know the saying -- if it sounds too good to be true, it probably is.

Take charge of your money. If you don't know where it goes, start keeping track. There are plenty of tools to help you set a monthly budget and stick to it.

Pay yourself first. Put yourself at the top of your "payee" list. Regular automatic deductions from your paycheck or bank account into a savings or investment account will keep you on track toward your short and long-term financial goals.

Know your investment self. You're the best judge of yourself. Use that knowledge to find investments that are a good match for you, based on your goals and your ability to tolerate risks.

Make sure your older investments still fit you. Take time to review your holdings and see if they're still appropriate for you. If you've outgrown them, it's probably time to sell them and buy something better suited to you.

Don't put all your eggs in one basket. One way to reduce the risks of investing is to diversify your investment holdings. Think twice before investing heavily in shares of your employer's stock or any single investment.

Ignorance isn't always bliss, especially when it comes to your account statements. Sure, it can hurt to look at statements when investments are losing value. But if you don't review your statements, you may miss problems in your accounts that are unrelated to performance.

Do your homework. Asking questions about financial opportunities and checking out the answers with unbiased sources can help you make informed choices and avoid fraud.

Other Investments

There are many other investments: real estate, precious metals, rare stamps and coins, stocks, bonds, special funds, and rare collectables. Investments of this type are difficult to understand without professional help, and cannot be addressed here.

Regardless of what you invest in, begin today.

# Part 6:
# Final Preparation

# Line of Duty Death

Many Police deaths are preventable. I just wrote something that will not be popular. Many police deaths are due to absolute stupidity. I just wrote something that will make me hated by some officers.

Driving at 110 miles per hour in a police car, on the way home, without a seatbelt is stupid and illegal. Every year we lose as many cops to accidents and crashes as we do to shootings.

There is no need to drive over 60 to any police call except for an officer calling for emergency assistance. Even then, I think 70 is the maximum. Driving at 90 or 100 will not shave that much off the response time, and the possibility that other backups may have to divert to help an office in a crash is great. If the officer crashes, he won't get there anyway, so slowing down a bit isn't so terrible.

Pursuits

According to the IACP, 1/3 of all pursuits end in a crash. 12% of all pursuits end in an injury or death. Over 300 deaths and thousands of injuries per year are directly connected with pursuits.

Driver draining is something most cops fail to request. An officer should have some type of driver training every four years. We drive every day, but we do not train for driving. We shoot our guns rarely in the line of duty, but we usually do train for shooting.

Bad tactics, bad equipment, lack of training, and other problems are not always the fault of the department. Here are the 10 Ten Deadly Errors of Law Enforcement and Police work, one more time. Read them as if your life depends on it!

## The 10 Ten Deadly Errors of Law Enforcement and Police Work

**1. LACK OF CONCENTRATION**: If you fail to keep your mind on the job while on patrol or carry home problems into the field, you start to make errors. It can cost you and your fellow officers their lives.

**2. TOMBSTONE COURAGE**: Just what it says, if time allows wait for backup. There are very few instances where you should try and make a dangerous apprehension unaided.

**3. NOT ENOUGH REST**: To do your job you must be alert. Lack of sleep or being sleepy can endanger yourself, the community and fellow officers.

**4. TAKING A BAD POSITION**: Never let anyone you are questioning or about to stop get in a better position than you are. There is no such animal as a routine stop!

**5. NOT HEEDING DANGER SIGNS**: As a cop you will get to recognize "danger signs". Movements, strange cars, warnings that should alert you to watch your step and approach with caution. Know your beat and watch for what is out of place.

**6. FAILURE TO WATCH THE HANDS OF A SUSPECT**: Is he or she reaching for a weapon or getting ready to assault you? Where else can a potential killer strike from, but from their hands!

**7. RELAXING TOO SOON**: YES, the rut of false alarms, kids in the park after curfew, barking dog calls, traffic stops during daylight hours all become mundane in time. ALWAYS observe the activity. NEVER take any call as routine or just another false alarm. It could be your life on the line.

**8. IMPROPER HANDCUFFING**: Once you have made the arrest, handcuff the prisoner correctly! See that the hands that can kill you are safely secured.

**9. NO SEARCH OR POOR SEARCH**: There are too many places to hide a weapon that if you fail to search you are guilty of committing a crime against other officers that will have contact with your prisoner. Many people carry weapons and are able and ready to use them on you. Never assume that the next guy or the jailer will do a "good" search.

**10. DIRTY OF INOPERATIVE WEAPON**: Is your sidearm clean? How about the bullets? Did you clean your weapon since the last range day? Or have you even shot or practiced drawing your weapon recently? Can you hit your target in a combat situation? You must practice faithfully and religiously!

# Life After Retirement

The average Police Officer lives only 5 years after retirement. According to the Central Florida Police Stress Unit, "Suicide rates are high among retired officers. Retirement is not an easy transition for most people and even more difficult for Police Officers. Many Officers do not have skills for other types of employment and are unprepared for retirement.

Informational seminars and counseling should be made available to Officers as early as five years prior to retirement. Spouses and other family members should be included in such seminars." Most Police Officers simply cannot deal with the fact that they are no longer part of the "Thin Blue Line" between law and lawlessness.

The loss of camaraderie, the feeling they are no longer part of the elite, and the feeling of being left out

are enough to drive many retired
Police Officers to self destructive
habits such as drinking, gambling,
smoking, and in some cases, suicide.

# Death After Retirement

# Line of Duty
## Death Benefits

The following is a list of benefits available to survivors of law enforcement officers killed in the line of duty; it is recommended that officers familiarize themselves with this list and give a copy to both family members and the family attorney.

The Federal Bureau of Justice Assistance, Office of Justice Programs, Public Safety Officers' Benefits Program offers death benefits for survivors. PSOB provides a one-time benefit to eligible survivors of public safety officers whose deaths were the direct and proximate result of an injury sustained in the line of duty on or after September 29, 1976. For the current death benefit amount, visit the PSOB web site at www.psob.gov. PSOB also provides a one-time benefit to eligible public safety officers who were permanently and totally disabled as a result of a catastrophic injury sustained in the line of duty on or after

November 29, 1990. Injuries must permanently prevent officers from performing any gainful work in the future. For the current disability benefit amount, visit www.psob.gov.

We must not forget that survivors who are wounded have feelings of survivor's guilt, inadequacy, and impotence.

PSOB provides support for higher education to eligible spouses and children of public safety officers who died in the line of duty on or after January 1, 1978, or were catastrophically disabled in the line of duty on or after October 3, 1996. For the current maximum educational assistance amount per month, visit www.psob.gov.

The following checklist is provided to streamline the PSOB filing process for the fallen officer's survivors. Call the PSOB Office for assistance with part of the PSOB claim.

The benefits coordinator must collect the information regarding the officer's line of duty death from agency records.

Among the records needed are the PSOB Report of Public Safety Officer's Death form, which must be completed and signed by the head of the police agency or designee, a detailed Statement of Circumstances from the initiation of the incident to the pronouncement of the officer's death, investigation, incident, and accident reports, if any.

In addition, the death certificate, autopsy report, and toxicology report, or a statement signed by the head of the public safety agency or designee explaining that none were performed.

Collect the information regarding the officer's survivor's beneficiaries. E-mail fax, or mail the above information to the PSOB Office, and keep a complete copy for your records.

The PSOB Claim for Death Benefits form should be completed and signed by the survivor/ claimant. Obtain the officer's current Marriage Certificate, if applicable. Obtain divorce decrees for the officer's and current spouse's previous marriages, including references to physical custody of any children, if applicable.

Obtain death certificates for the officer's and current spouse's previous marriages, if any of the marriages ended in death, if applicable. Obtain birth certificates for all the officer's surviving children and step-children, regardless of age or dependency, identifying the children's parents, if applicable.

Contact Public Safety Officers' Benefits Office, Bureau of Justice Assistance, Office of Justice Programs, at 810 Seventh Street NW. Fourth Floor Washington, DC 20531 Phone: 202–307–0635 Toll-free: 1–888–744–6513 E-mail: AskPSOB@usdoj.gov PSOB web site: www.psob.gov

Law Enforcement Officers who are NRA members, killed in the line of duty, will have $25,000 in life insurance coverage. E-mail membership@nrahq.org. or contact the NRA via mail at the following address:

National Rifle Association of America, 11250 Waples Mill Road, Fairfax, VA 22030. Contact the NRA via phone at: NRA Member Programs, 1-800-672-3888.

The PBA or FOP offers a cash donation to families of PBA or FOP members killed in the line of duty. For more information contact The Police Benevolent Association or Fraternal Order of Police.

The county or department may provide certain death and pension benefits pursuant to the applicable FOP or PBA contract and the Employee Manual.

The state may pay benefits as well. The State of Florida pursuant to F.S. 112.19 pays to the beneficiary designated by officer during life and delivered by state. Other states may offer like benefits. Florida pays $59,694.46 if death is accidental, $59,694.46 if death is accidental and officer was in "fresh pursuit" or responding to an emergency, or

$179,083.29 if unlawfully and intentionally killed.

The State of Florida pursuant to F.S. 112.193 provides that upon the death of law enforcement officer, the employer may present to the spouse or other beneficiary of the officer, upon request, one complete uniform, including the badge worn by the officer. However, if law enforcement officer is killed in the line of duty, the employer may present, upon request, to the spouse or other beneficiary of the officer the officer's service-issued handgun, if one was issued as part of the officer's equipment.

If the employer is not in possession of the service-issued handgun, the employer may, within its discretion, and upon written request of the spouse or other beneficiary, present a similar handgun.

The State of Florida pursuant to F.S.440.16 pays compensation for death, if death results from the accident within 1 year thereafter or follows continuous disability and results from the accident within 5 years thereafter, the employer shall pay: (a) Within 14 days after receiving the bill, actual funeral expenses not to exceed $7,500.

The State of Florida pursuant to F.S.440.16 (b) pays compensation, in addition to the above, in the following percentages of the average weekly wages to the following persons entitled thereto on account of dependency upon the deceased, and in the following order of preference, subject to the limitation provided in subparagraph 2., but such compensation shall be subject to the limits provided in s. 440.12(2), shall not exceed $150,000, and may be less than, but shall not exceed, for all dependents or persons entitled to compensation, 662/3 percent of the average wage to the spouse, if there is no child, 50 percent of the average weekly
wage, such compensation to cease
upon the spouse's death.

Contact the Division of Workers Compensation: Division of Workers'

Compensation Assessments Unit, 200 East Gaines Street, Tallahassee, FL 32399-4221, (800) 219-8953

The State of Florida pursuant to F.S. 112.19 2(3) states that if a law enforcement officer is accidentally killed or unlawfully and intentionally killed the state shall waive certain educational expenses that the child or spouse of the deceased officer incurs while obtaining a career certificate, an undergraduate education, or a postgraduate education.

The amount waived by the state shall be an amount equal to the cost of tuition and matriculation and registration fees for a total of 120 credit hours. The child or spouse may attend a state career center, a state community college, or a state university. The child or spouse may attend any or all of the institutions specified in this subsection, on either a full-time or part-time basis.

The benefits provided to a child under this subsection shall continue until the child's 25th birthday. The benefits provided to a spouse under this subsection must commence within 5 years after the death occurs, and entitlement thereto shall continue until the 10$^{th}$ anniversary of that death. The waiver can be obtained from the registrar of the school the child attends.

The State of Florida pursuant to F.S. 440.16 (c) pays to the surviving spouse, payment of postsecondary student fees for instruction at any career center up to 1,800 classroom hours or payment of student fees at any community college established under part III of chapter 1004 for up to 80 semester hours. The spouse of a deceased state employee shall be entitled to a full waiver of such fees. The benefits provided for in this paragraph shall be in addition to other benefits provided for in this section and shall terminate 7 years after the death of the deceased employee, or when the total payment in eligible compensation under paragraph (b) has been received.

The State of Florida pursuant to F.S. 112.19(h)1 provides that any employer who employs a full-time law enforcement officer who suffers a catastrophic injury, in the line of duty shall pay the entire premium of the employer's health insurance plan for the injured employee, the injured employee's spouse, and for each dependent child of the injured employee until the child reaches the age of majority or until the end of the calendar year in which the child reaches the age of 25.

If the child continues to be dependent for support, or the child is a full-time or part-time student and is dependent for support. The term "health insurance plan" does not include supplemental benefits that are not part of the basic group health insurance plan. If the injured employee subsequently dies, the employer shall continue to pay the entire health insurance premium for the surviving spouse until remarried, and for the dependent children, under the conditions outlined in this paragraph.

There exists a "Dignity Memorial Funeral, Cremation and Cemetery Providers created the Public Servants Program" for emergency service personnel. This program provides dignified and honorable tributes, at no cost, for career and volunteer law enforcement officers who fall in the line of duty. Visit their website for complete information at www.dignitymemorial.com and look under Public Servants for details. Call 800-344-6489.

## Concerns of Police Survivors, Inc.

COPS is a national, non-profit organization that works with law enforcement agencies, police organizations, mental health professionals, and local peer-support organizations to provide assistance to surviving families of law enforcement officers killed in the line of duty.

COPS has become a "lifeline" to police survivors nationwide. Contact the COPS National Office at

www.nationalcops.org/chap.htm
or at
P.O. Box 3199
3096 S. State Highway 5
Camdenton, MO 65020
Phone: 573-346-4911
Fax: 573-346-1414

According to TASER Foundation (2011). The TASER Foundation distributes financial gifts to the families of fallen officers in the U.S. and Canada through donations and an initial endowment of $1,000,000 that was created by TASER International and the direct contributions from TASER International employees. Grants are available only upon request by the chiefs of police and sheriffs as well as federal law enforcement executives in the name of officers killed in the line of duty since August 1, 2004 going forward.

TASER International, Inc. bears all of the administrative costs of the TASER Foundation in order to ensure 100 percent of all donations are distributed to the families of fallen officers. The TASER Foundation is a 501(c)3 tax exempt corporation. All donations are tax deductible to the extent allowable by law.

To protect and serve - every day over 850,000 law enforcement officers in the United States and Canada work to fulfill this mission. Sometimes these officers make the ultimate sacrifice and are tragically killed in the line of duty.

In 2004, 153 officers in the United States and 7 in Canada were tragically killed in the line of duty. Over 6,000 law enforcement agencies have lost officers in the line of duty. The average age of an officer lost in the line of duty is only 38 years old.

In response to these tragedies, and as a way to give back to the law enforcement community, TASER® International, Inc. established the TASER Foundation in November 2004. The initial endowment of $1,000,000 came from TASER International, Inc. and the direct contributions from TASER International employees.

As of December 31, 2004 the TASER Foundation has awarded $188,500 to the families of fallen law enforcement officers in the United States and Canada. Please donate to this worthy cause. Visit their website at:

www.taser.com.

"This train _will_ stop at Tucumcari."

~ Lee Van Cleef

# Officer's Wishes

# Sample Form

**Name:** _____

**Date:**_____

Update:_____          Update:_____

Update:_____          Update:_____

Update:_____          Update:_____

Update:_____          Update:_____

## ORGAN DONATION

☐ I do not want any of my organs donated.

☐ I would like to have organs donated for transplant.

☐ I would like to donate the following organs for transplant/research:

---

## FUNERAL DETAILS

Church Preference: _____

Religious Affiliation: _____

Clergyman: _____

Phone: _____

Funeral Home to be used:

_____

Phone: _____

I have a pre-paid burial plan. Yes ☐ No ☐

Contact: _____


Service to be held at:

Funeral Home _____

 Name of Funeral Home: _____

Church _____

Name of Church:
_____

I prefer:

Interment ☐ Entombment ☐ Cremation ☐

My choice of cemetery is:
_____

☐ I have purchased a lot. ☐ I have not purchased a lot.




Lot is in name of:
_____

Section _____

Lot _____    _____

Block _____

Location of deed for lot:

_____

If interment is in another city, give information on the
receiving funeral home:

Name: _____

Phone: _____

Address: _____

Pallbearers:

_____

_____

_____

_____

_____

_____

If cremated, what do you wish done with your ashes?

_____
_____

Obituary: Yes ☐ No ☐

Please list the following in my obituary:

_____
_____
_____
_____

I am entitled to Veterans Benefits: Yes ☐ No ☐

I entitled to Military Honors: Yes ☐ No ☐

I would like a "Lodge" service: Yes ☐ No ☐

By:

_____
_____

Flowers: Yes ☐ No ☐

Disposal of flowers: _____

Donations in lieu of flowers to:

_____

Musical selections:

_____
_____
_____

Special requests for service:

_____
_____
_____

## SPECIAL FINAL REQUESTS

Special final requests should be addressed in one's will so your wishes will be upheld by a court of law. If you have not addressed these special final requests in a will, your primary beneficiary will have total control of your assets/possessions for final disposal. We strongly recommend addressing these issues in your will. If you choose not to, however, complete this section to alleviate your family of the decisions that might need to be made in your behalf.

This is how I would like insurance settlement money to be spent:

_____
_____
_____
_____

This is how I would like real estate to be handled:

_____
_____
_____
_____
_____
_____

## MY LIVING WILL

Individuals may execute a "living will" that instructs family members and physicians to not take extraordinary steps to continue your life on life-support machines. You should investigate the legality of the "living will" within your state and take steps to execute the "living will" if you do not chose to be kept alive through mechanical means.

☐ I have not executed a "living will"

☐ I have executed a "living will"

Since copies of living wills may not be acceptable in some states, an ***original, signed***

copy of my living will is readily accessible at:

_____

☐ Additional copies of my "living will" are on file with my personal physician, attorney, and with my will.

## MY WILL

Your will should address special requests on how you would like insurance money to be spent, who you would like to have your prized possessions, etc. By providing this information in a will, your wishes can be upheld in court. Otherwise, your primary beneficiary will have total control of your assets/possessions. However, if this information is not included in your will, there is a section in this handbook for that information to be provided.

256

I do not have a will. ☐ (Often times families incur additional emotional, legal and financial burdens when a loved one dies without having executed a will.

I have a will that is located at:

_____

The Attorney who handled my will is

_____

at the law firm of

_____

Phone number: _____

My last will is dated:

_____

The Executor is:

_____

## POLICE FUNERALS

Social Security Number: _____

Date of Birth: _____

In case of death or serious injury, have a department representative contact:

Spouse:

_____

Mother:

_____

Father:

_____

Close Relative:

_____

Close Relative:

_____

Close Relative:

_____


Former Spouse(s):

_____

My best friend on the department is

_____
and I would like him (her) to accompany anyone sent to give
injury/death notice to my family. My best friend's address is:

_____

Phone number

_____

The following members of my family have health concerns
that the department should be aware of:

_____

_____

My family is aware of the beneficiaries listed on all my
department insurance forms.

Yes ☐ No ☐

I have a letter written to my family explaining why I have
named certain beneficiaries on my policies. Yes ☐ No ☐

I would like full law enforcement honors if killed in the line of
duty. Yes ☐ No ☐

Suggested departmental pallbearers:

_____
_____
_____
_____

☐ Or standard honor guard pallbearers.

## PERSONAL DOCUMENTS/INFORMATION

My birth date is:

_____

My birth certificate is located at:

_____

I was born in:

_____

My social security number:

_____

Marriage 1:

I was married in:

_____

On:

_____

To:

_____

Children from this marriage:

_____

Children from this marriage:

_____

I was divorced on:

_____

State of:

_____

## Marriage 2:

I was married in:

_____

On:

_____

To:

_____

Children from this marriage:

_____

Children from this marriage:

_____

I was divorced on:

_____

State of:

_____

Marriage 3:

I was married in:

_____

On:

_____

To:

_____

Children from this marriage:

_____

Children from this marriage:

_____

I was divorced on:

_____

State of:

_____


Current Marriage certificate(s) are located at:

_____

Divorce decree(s) are located at:

_____

Children's birth certificates are located at:

_____

Children's adoption papers are located at:

_____

I served in the Armed Forces: Branch:

_____

Service Serial Number:

_____

Enlisted on:

_____

At: _____

Discharge Date:

_____

Discharge papers located at:

_____

# References

29 U.S.C. §§ 201

29 U.S.C. § 254(a)

Alderfer, C. (1969). An empirical test of a new
    theory of human needs. Organizational
    Behavior and Human Performance, 4,
    142–175.

Alderfer, C. (1972). *Existence, Relatedness, &*
    *Growth*. New York: Free Press.

American Academy of Sleep Medicine (2001).
    "The International Classification of Sleep
    Disorders, Revised: Diagnostic and   Coding
Manual". 2001 edition, Retrieved      on September
05, 2009 from:           www.absm.org

Anakwe, U.P., & Greenhaus, J.H. (1999).
    Effective socialization of employees:
    Socialization content perspective. Journal
    of Managerial Issues. 11 (3), 315-329.

Article II, Section 8, Florida Constitution

Ashforth, B., & Saks, A. (1996). Socialization
    tactics: Longitudinal effects on
    newcomer adjustment. Academy of
    Management Journal, 39 (1), 149-178.

Best, S. and Kellner, D. (2001), The Postmodern
    Adventure, New York and London:

Guilford Press and Routledge.


Boisnier, A. and Chatman, J. (2002). The Role
of Subcultures in Agile Organizations.
CA: University of California, Berkeley.

Brooks, P. (1976 ) Officer down, code three.
Northbrook, IL: Motorola Teleprograms
Inc.

Bivens v. Six Unknown Named Agents, 403 U.S.
388 (1971)

Brower v. County of Inyo, 489 U.S. 593 (1989)


Cable, D., & Parsons C. (2001). Socialization
tactics and person-organization fit.
Personnel Psychology, 54 (1), 1-23.

Campbell, J. P. (1990). Modeling the
performance prediction problem in
industrial and  organizational psychology.
In M. D. Dunnette & L. M. Hough (Eds.),
Handbook of Industrial and rganizational
Psychology (pp. 687-732). Palo Alto, CA:
Consulting Psychologists Press, Inc.;

Campbell,  J.P.,  &  Campbell,  R.J.  (1988).
Productivity  in  Organizations:  New
perspectives  from  industrial  and
organizational  psychology.  San
Francisco: Jossy-Bass.

Campbell, J.P., Dunnette, M.D., Lawler, E.E., &
    Weick, K.E. (1970). Managerial behavior,
    performance, and effectiveness. New
    York: McGraw-Hill.

CBP Employment Opportunities - Border Patrol
    Agent.  Retrieved October 31, 2009
    from:  www.usborderpatrol.gov/

Champoux, J. E.  (2006).  Organizational
    behavior: Integrating individuals, groups,
    And Organizations.  Miami, OH:
    Thomson/South-Western.

Chao, G, O'Leary-Kelly A., Wolf, S. Klein, H.,
    and Gardner P. (1994).  Organizational
    Socialization:  Its Content and
    Consequences.  Journal of Applied
    Psychology, 79  (5), 730-743.

*City of Canton, Ohio v. Harris, 109 S. Ct. 1197
(1989).*

Civil Rights Act of 1871

"Criminal   Justice   Professionalism   Program".
    Retrieved December 09, 2009, from
    http://www.fdle.state.fl.us/Content/getdoc/4
    44bc020-4c94-4674-bb87-
    207089dd319a/Overview-of-the-
    Professionalism-Program.aspx

Dade Co. v. Alvarez, 124 F.3d 1380, 1997
    U.S.App. Lexis 28604 (11th Cir.). [1996
    FP      42 & 1998 FP 7]

Davidson, A. (2005).   Killer Game Programming
in Java.  Sebastopol, CA.  O'Reilly
Media, Inc.

Daniels, M. (1982). The development of the
concept of self-actualization in the
writings of Abraham Maslow. *Current
Psychological Reviews, 2*. 61-76.

"Durkheim's Anomie" Retrieved December 22,
2009, from
http://www.criminology.fsu.edu/crimtheo
ry/week8.htm

El Paso County Sheriff's Office Policy and
Procedure Manual. Colorado Springs,
Colorado, USA: El    Paso County
Sheriff's Office. 2004-01-01.

ERG Theory - Clayton P. Alderfer.  Retrieved
December 13, 2009 from:
http://www.valuebasedmanagement.net/m
ethods_alderfer_erg_theory.html

Expectancy Theory - Victor Vroom.  Retrieved
December 13, 2009 from:
http://www.valuebasedmanagement.net/m
ethods_vroom_expectancy_theory.html

Field  Training  Officers  Program.  Based  Upon
The San Jose, California Model. Public
Agency Training Council.    Retrieved
October 14, 2009 from:

http://www.patc.com/training/brochures/2009/8072.pdf

Finn, P. (1997). Reducing Stress - An Organization Centered Approach. FBI Law Enforcement Bulletin. August 1997. Retrieved November 4, 2009 from: http://www.policestress.org/suicide.htm.

"Florida Commission on Ethics". Retrieved December 15, 2009, from http://www.ethics.state.fl.us/

Florida Department of Law Enforcement. Retrieved October 14, 2009 from: www.fdle.state.fl.us/.

Florida State Statute 11.062(2)

Florida State Statute 119.01

Florida State Statute 287

Florida State Statute 316.1925

Florida State Statute 316.192

Florida State Statute 350.031

Florida State Statute 350.05

Florida State Statute 350.0605

Gagliardi, P. 1986. The creation and change of organizational cultures: A conceptual

framework. Organization Studies, 72:
117-134.

Garrity v. New Jersey, 385 U.S. 493 (1967)

Gates, D. (1992). *Chief: My Life in the LAPD*.
New York: Bantam.

Herzberg, F. (1968). One more time: How do you
Motivate Employees? *Harvard
Business Review 46*, 53–62.

Herzberg, F., Mausner, B. & Snyderman, B.B.
(1959), *The Motivation to Work*. John
Wiley. New York.

Hofstede , G. Motivation, leadership, and
organization: Do American theories apply
abroad?  Organizational Dynamics, 1980

Huitt, W. (2007). Maslow's hierarchy of needs.
*Educational Psychology Interactive*.
Valdosta, GA: Valdosta State University.
Retrieved  December 13, 2009  from:
http://www.edpsycinteractive.org/topics/r
egsys/maslow.html

Institute for Management Excellence. (2001).
The nine basic human needs. *Online
Newsletter*. Retrieved December 13,  2009,
from:
http://www.itstime.com/print/jun97p.htm

Kirsh, D. (2001). 'The Context of Work'.    Human
Computer Interaction.  2001

Law Enforcement Suicide: The Hidden Epidemic. Retrieved October 14, 2009 from: http://www.policestress.org/suicide.htm

Law Enforcement Training Reference Guide (2011). Retrieved February 17, 2009 from: http://pursuitpolicy.org/?p=408

Legal Representation. Retrieved on November 11, 2009 from: http://www.flpba.org

Lloyd, J. (2000). "Change in tactics: Police trade talk for rapid response". The Christian Science Monitor. 05-31-2000.

Maslow, A. (1943). A Theory of Human Motivation. Psychological Review, 50(4), 370- 396.

Minnesota Multiphasic Personality Inventory-2 (MMPI-2). Retrieved October 14, 2009 From: www.pearsonassessments.com/

Muchinsky, P.M., (2003). Psychology applied to work. Belmont, CA: Thompson-Wadsworth.

Nohria, N., Lawrence, P., & Wilson, E. (2001). *Driven: How human nature shapes our choices*. San Francisco: Jossey-Bass.

Norwood, G. (1999). Maslow's hierarchy of needs. *The Truth Vectors* (Part I). Retrieved December 13, 2009 from:

http://www.deepermind.com/20maslow.htm

NTOA History. Retrieved December 3, 2009 from: www.ntoa.org

Ohio Trainer Makes The Case For Single-Officer Entry Against Active Killers. Retrieved December 10, 2009 from: http://en.wikipedia.org/wiki/Active_shooter - cite_ref- 2http://www.policeone.com/active-shooter/articles/1695125-Ohio-trainer-makes-the-case-for-single-officer-entry-against-active-killers/

Oldham, G. & Cummings, A. (1997). Enhancing creativity: managing work contexts for the high potential employee. California Management Review: University of California Press.

OSHA fact sheet. What is workplace violence? U.S. Department of Labor Occupational Safety and Health Administration 2002.

Ostroff, C., & Kozlowski, S. (1992). Organizational socialization as a learning process:The role of information acquisition. Personnel Psychology, 45, 849-874.

Our History. Retrieved December 3, 2009 from: www.hpoadade.org

Pipes, C. (2001). Police pursuits and civil liability. *FBI law enforcement bulletin.*

"Professional Compliance (Disciplinary) Process". Retrieved December 09, 2009, from http://www.fdle.state.fl.us/Content/getdoc/f7 de3350-3b11-4917-8f98- e0532f4761ba/Professional- Compliance.aspx

Provenzo, E.F. (1986). "Beyond the Gutenberg Galaxy: Micro Computers and the Emergence of Post-Typographic Culture." New York, NY: Teachers College Press.

Rugala, E. ed. (2003) Workplace Violence Issues In Response. Quantico, Virginia:     FBI Academy. Critical Incident Response     Group National Center for the Analysis of Violent Crime.

Sacramento v. Lewis, 523 U.S. 833 (1998)

Scanlon, J. (2001). "Active Shooter Situations: What do we do now?!!". North American SWAT Training Association. July/August 2001. Vol. XXVI No. 4. Retrieved on February 12, 2011 from: http://www.nasta.ws/police_marksman.htm.

Scott v. Harris, 550 U.S. 372 (2007)

Suicide: Retrieved October 14, 2009 from: http://www.policestress.org/suicide.htm.

Sundermeier, J. (2009) A Look at the 12-Hour
    Shift: The Lincoln Police Department
    Study.  he Police Chief, vol. 75, no. 3,
    March 2008.

Taormina, R.J. (1994). The Organizational
    Socialization Inventory. International
    Journal  of Selection and Assessment, 2,
    133-145.

Tennessee v. Garner, 471 U.S. 1 (1985)

The Bible, New Testament. Book of the
    Revelation of John.

The  NOBLE  Purpose.  Retrieved  December  3,
    2009 from:  www.noblenatl.org

The    Portal-to-Portal    Act.    Retrieved    on
    November    11,    2009    from:
    http://www.dol.gov/

The Seven Categories of Drugs.
http://www.decp.org/experts/7categories.htm

"The  "Sunshine"  Law".  Retrieved  December  15,
    2009, from
    http://www.myflsunshine.com/sun.nsf/pa
    ges/Law.

Tips for 2011.  Retrieved on February 21, 2011
    from: http://www.sec.gov/index.htm.

Trice, H.M., & Beyer, J. M. 1984. Studying
    organizational cultures through rites and

ceremonials Academy of Management
Review, 9: 653-669.


Two Factor Theory - Herzberg, Frederick.
Retrieved December 13, 2009
from: http://www.valuebasedmanagement
.net/methods_herzberg_two_factor_theor
y.html


U.S. Department of Justice Americans with
Disabilities Act. Retrieved October 31,
2009 from: www.ada.gov/

U.S. Equal Employment Opportunity
Commission (EEOC). Retrieved October
14, 2009 from: www.eeoc.gov/

Van Maanen, J. (1978). People processing:
strategies of organizational socialization.
Organizational Dynamics. 7 (1), 1936.

Violanti, J. (2008). Law Enforcement Suicide:
The Hidden Epidemic. Retrieved October
14, 2009. from:
http://www.policestress.org/suicide.htm.

*"Tous les jours à tous points de vue je vais de mieux en mieux"*

"Every day in every way I am getting better and better"


~ Émile Coué

# NOTES

# NOTES

# NOTES

# NOTES

# NOTES

# NOTES

WHITE MOUNTAIN PUBLISHING CO.

MIAMI, FLORIDA

2011

Printed in Great Britain
by Amazon